India

Front cover: Mehrangarh Fort in Jodhpur at sunrise

Right: A traditional mode of transport

TOP 10 ATTRACTIONS

Hampi. The deserted Vijayanagar capital is perhaps India's most evocative ruin. See page 197.

Jaisalmer. The desert citadel has a golden sandstone fort and wonderful old town houses. See page 122.

Ladakh. Where Buddhist monasteries hug the hills. See page 105.

Madurai. Famed for the Meenakshi temple, with its brightly coloured and towering gopuras. See page 186.

Agra. Location of the Taj Mahal and other Mughal wonders, including nearby Fatehpur Sikri. See page 77.

Khajuraho. Hindu temples festooned with erotic sculpture. See page 144.

Kerala's backwaters. The palm-lined backwaters represent tropical India at its most intense. See page 187.

Varanasi. The bathing ghats of this sacred city present an unforgettable spectacle. See page 90.

Ajanta and Ellora. Superb frescoes and sculpture adorn these breathtaking cave temples. See page 137 and 139.

The Golden Temple. The Sikhs' holiest shrine in the city of Amritsar ranks alongside the Taj for its ethereal architecture. See page 96.

A PERFECT TOUR

Day 1 — Old Delhi

Start at Shah Jahan's implacable Red Fort, former seat of the great Mughal emperors. Recover from the sightseeing with lunch, then visit the red-sandstone Jama Masjid mosque for a matchless view over the surrounding rooftops. After supper, catch a Bollywood blockbuster at a multiplex on Connaught Circus.

Day 2 — South Delhi

The crumbling 15th-century Afghan tombs in Lodi Gardens provide a superbly atmospheric spot for an early-morning limber up. Afterwards, browse the antique shops, hip clothes boutiques, art galleries and ethnic jewellery stalls jammed into the old alleyways of Hauz Khas village. Spend the afternoon exploring Humayun's Tomb and the Qutb Minar complex.

Day 3 — Agra

Arrive at the Taj Mahal in time to catch sunrise over the splendid white marble mausoleum, and return in the evening to see how striking it is at sunset. Spend the period between visits to the Taj taking in nearby Agra Fort, the tomb of Itimad-ud-Daulah and Akbar's fabulous mausoleum at Sikandra, where monkeys and gazelle graze in the grounds.

Day 4 — Fatehpur Sikri

An early start is recommended for a trip to Akbar's ghost town, whose sandstone domes and walkways glow terracotta-red in the morning light. Begin at the palace complex and Diwan-i-Am and wind up at the impressive Jama Masjid mosque, where the white marble Tomb of Sheikh Salim Chishti provides an exquisite finale.

OF INDIA

Day 6 Ranthambore

The Rajput ruins, forest and lake shores of Ranthambore offer the most romantic backdrop imaginable for sighting wild tigers. Between safaris, join a village tour to see more of the local life.

Day 7 Pushkar

Spend the day skirting arid southern Rajasthan to reach the holy Hindu pilgrimage town of Pushkar, whose whitewashed domes, temples and ghats rise from an exquisite lake in the desert. Dine on a rooftop overlooking the water as the sun sets and the sound of puja bells fill the air.

Day 9 Jaipur

A ride on elephant back to the gateway of Amber Fort is an irresistible way to start a day in the Rajasthani capital. After lunch, visit the resplendent City Palace complex, with its collection of Mughal and Rajput costume, carpets and weapons, winding up at the Palace of Winds for a fine view over the bazaar.

Day 5 Bharatpur

Base yourself in Bharatpur to experience birding safaris at the rich wetlands of Keoladeo National Park, which is best visited by bicycle. Expect glimpses of man-sized Saras cranes, flamingos and pelicans.

Day 8 Ajmer

For a matchless view of the town and surrounding sand hills, set off at first light to climb the ancient stepway leading to the Savitri temple on a hilltop to the south of Pushkar. Just over the mountain, Ajmer is the site of the most sacred Sufi shrine in India, the marble tomb of medieval mystic Khwaja Muin-ud-din Chishti. A time-worn pathway leads from behind it to the ruined Taragarh Fort – another spectacular viewpoint.

CONTENTS

INTRODUCTION

No place for the faint-hearted, India is a constant challenge to mind and body; a glorious shock to the system. It is exhilarating, exhausting and infuriating; a land where, you will find, the practicalities of daily life overlay the mysteries of popular myth. In place of the much-publicised, and much-misunderstood, mysticism of its ancient religions, India in reality has quite another miracle to offer in the sheer profusion of its peoples and landscapes.

The country comprises a diamond-shaped subcontinent that stretches over 3,000km (1,800 miles) from the Himalayas in the north right down to Kanyakumari, or Cape Comorin, on the Indian Ocean. From east to west India also covers about 3,000km, from Arunachal Pradesh and Assam on the border with its neighbours China and Myanmar (Burma), to the Gujarat coast on the Arabian Sea. The topography extends from the snow of the high Himalayas, to the deserts of Rajasthan, to the lush tropical landscape of Kerala.

Only in more recent post-colonial times did its natural geography exclude the neighbouring countries of Pakistan and Bangladesh, where, for all the hostilities, there's an undeniable cultural affinity with India. The enormity of India itself means there are different and inevitably conflicting regional and sectarian interests. India boasts no less than 22 official languages: Hindi, Urdu, Sanskrit, Sindhi, Bengali, Marathi, Gujarati, Oriya, Maithili, Santhali, Dogri, Punjabi, Assamese, Bodo, Manipuri, Nepali, Kashmiri, Malayalam, Konkani, Kannada, Tamil and Telugu; an estimated 850 languages are in daily use. The official national language is Hindi, much to the disgust of the Tamils, but it is spoken by far less than the majority. English, still much used by government and institutions, is spoken by just five percent of the people, mostly in the south and larger cities.

The incomparable Taj Mahal

One of the first impressions you'll get at the airport in Delhi or Mumbai (Bombay) is the diversity of India's peoples. From green-eyed and sometimes light brown-haired Kashmiris and Tibetans, through the Indo-European-speaking peoples of northern and central India, right down to dark-skinned Dravidians from the south, you soon realise there's no such thing as a 'typical' Indian. India's prehistoric settlers were probably what anthropologists call Proto-Australoids. They have since been joined by Mongols, Aryans, Greeks, Arabs, Turks, Persians and Afghans, while Dutch, British, Portuguese and French have also left their traces.

Landscape and heritage

The landscape is alternately rich and arid, lush and desolate. In the Hindu scriptures, Shiva, one of the most revered Hindu gods is said to live in the fittingly majestic Himalayas in the north of India. Kashmir is a beautiful and coveted land of green forest, alpine meadows and lakes, while the Punjab in the northwest is the

Picking tea, Darjeeling

fertile centre of the country's Green Revolution, supporting the nation's self-sufficiency in wheat, barley and millet. On the doorstep of this wealth, the Thar Desert of Rajasthan heralds the vast Deccan plateau of parched, ruddy granite that dominates the peninsula of southern India.

Delhi stands at the western end of the Ganges river basin in which India grows much of its rice. Flanked with patches of forest leading up into the foothills of the Himalayas, the flat plain stretches right across to the Bay of Bengal 1,600km (1,000 miles) away, but some

Amar Singh Pol gate in Agra Fort

areas are kept as nature reserves for the country's wildlife, notably its tigers, leopards and elephants. Bengal's greenery is the threshold to the tea plantations of Darjeeling and Assam.

The rugged southern peninsula is hemmed in by low-lying mountains; the Vindhya and Satpura to the north and the Western and Eastern Ghats running parallel to the coasts. The forested Malabar coast in the west is sown with crops of coconut, betel nut, pepper, cardamom, rubber and cashew nut, which today still tempt ships across the Arabian Sea. Palm trees line the shores all the way around peninsular India, from Mumbai to the Ganges delta.

India's landscape also features man-made architectural treasures, bearing witness to the many great religions and civilisations that have enriched the country. After centuries of neglect, these monuments are now preserved by the restoration programme run by the Archaeological Survey of India. The sights are endless: the Hindu *gopura* (temple towers) of the south; the *ghats* of Varanasi (Benares); the cave monasteries of Ajanta and Ellora; the beautiful and erotic sculptures of Khajuraho; the splendid marble palaces, fortresses and mausoleums of the emperors and maharajas in Delhi, Agra and Rajasthan; the colonial government buildings in New Delhi; and the unusual style of the gothic-oriental municipal piles in Mumbai.

People

The only constant in this huge landscape is the presence of people themselves. Even in the vast open spaces of the Rajasthan desert or the Deccan plateau of central India, people appear everywhere: a tribesman on camel-back or a lone woman holding her headdress in her teeth to keep out the dust as she carries a huge pitcher of water or a bundle of firewood on her head. If, as the road stretches before you empty and clear right up to the horizon, you can see only one tree, there's a good chance you'll find at least one *sadhu* (holy man) resting in its shade.

The teeming millions living in Delhi, Mumbai and Kolkata have become legendary. They crowd each other into the roadway,

Some statistics

India's area of 3,287,590 sq km (1,269,346 sq miles) makes it the seventh-largest country in the world, but it has the world's second-largest population (after China).

Capital: Delhi, pop. 11,007,835.

Major cities: Mumbai (Bombay), pop. 12,478,447; Kolkata (Calcutta), pop. 4,486,679; Chennai (Madras), pop. 4,681,087; Bengaluru (Bangalore), pop. 8,425,970; Hyderabad, pop. 6,809,970; Ahmedabad, pop. 5,570,585; Surat, pop. 4,462,002.

Population: 1.21 billion, of whom roughly 72 percent are Indo-European, mostly in the north, 25 percent Dravidian in the south, 3 percent others. Density is 335 people per sq km (867 per sq mile).

Religion: about 79 percent Hindu, 14.6 percent Muslim, 2.3 percent Christian, 1.9 percent Sikh, 0.76 percent Buddhist, the remainder Jain and others.

The bustle of Delhi's Old City off Chandhi Chowk

bulge out of tiny auto-rickshaws, and perch on top of buses and trains; a family of four or five clings onto a motor-scooter, and a whole school class on one bullock-cart. It is hazardous: buses do topple over, rooftop passengers on trains do occasionally get swept off the top by an overhanging cable, but they accept the risk for the free ride. Despite impressive economic progress, there remain vast numbers of people living in absolute poverty, in the big cities as well as in rural areas. Traditionally borne with a kind of stoical resignation, poverty has, over the past decade or so, caused increasing social unrest. Unlike in the past where the disadvantaged classes rarely came into contract with those who were better off, modern life throws all sections of Indian society together. The result, exacerbated by the economic boom, is a growing sense of entitlement among the poor which has provoked mass marches and, in the most impoverished corners of central India, a full-blown uprising which now verges on the scale of a civil war.

Even so, most of the country remains remarkably peaceful considering how many people are packed cheek-by-jowl into its largest

A Hindu ceremony

cities. The resulting jostling may also be an alien concept to many visitors, but it's a way of life in India. The cities' *bastis* (shanty-town districts) are often directly in the shadow of the shining skyscrapers, built by the *basti*-dwellers themselves. Here women carry piles of bricks on their heads as gracefully as they would a pitcher of water. The women are also responsible for one other characteristic of the Indian landscape: cow-dung patties which are preserved and kept for fuel and artfully shaped into mounds. And everyone makes way for the cow, sacred to Hindus. The cow has right of way everywhere, whether walking nonchalantly through the centre of a city, or reclining across a new expressway. After a while you may begin to detect something a bit uncanny in the way a cow seems to look around and beyond her immediate surroundings; it's as if she *knows* that she's sacred.

Religions of India

You can't get around it: India is a country where religion is ever-present. Although the constitution of today describes India as a secular state, religion still plays a vital part in everyday life: in its streets as well as in the architecture, sculpture and painting of its great monuments.

Hinduism

More than 80 percent of the population embraces **Hinduism**, which is more a way of life than a religion; its sacred rituals and observances are only a small part of what good Hindus believe makes them good Hindus. Much more than the mystical elements which fascinate and draw so many Westerners here, Hinduism is concerned with the basics of everyday life: birth, work, health, relationships and death, all of this helped along by regular consultations with an astrologer. India's principal religion may therefore owe its popularity to the fact that it offers something for everyone: mysticism and metaphysics for scholars, ritual and spectacle for devotees, encompassing austerity, sensuality, tranquillity and frenzy.

Building on early indigenous belief systems and the Vedic teachings of the Indo-Aryans dating back to the second millennium BC, Hinduism began to take its present form in the 4th century AD, under considerable pressure for a more 'accessible' religion. Popular devotional worship, *bhakti*, with its appeal to a wide range of people, replaced the sacrifices practised exclusively by the Brahmins.

It is said there are 330 million gods in the Hindu pantheon, but they might be seen as 330 million facets of a single divinity.

Cows are sacred to Hindus

A statue of Vishnu

The three most important are Vishnu, Brahma and Shiva, often presented to Westerners as a trinity, though this is not really comparable to the Christian concept.

Vishnu is the preserver of the universe; a four-armed god with mace, conch, discus and lotus, he has many incarnations, of which the most famous is Krishna, who appears as conquering hero, flute-playing lover or mischievous baby. Vishnu's wife Lakshmi is goddess of wealth. Brahma is the creator of the world, self-born (without mother) in the lotus flower that grew from the navel of Vishnu at the beginning of the universe.

Shiva is the dancing destroyer-god, wearing a garland of skulls and snakes around both neck and arms. As the god of time and ascetics, he decides the fate of the world. As lord of beasts and king of dance, Shiva is as passionate as Vishnu is serene. Just in case you think you have got it all clear, remember that Shiva preserves through the renewal arising from destruction.

Hindu ethics assert that the path to salvation has three principles: righteousness; prosperity honestly achieved; and, not least, pleasure. At the centre of the confrontation with the harsh reality of daily life are the concepts of '*dharma*' and '*karma*'; that is 'correct' behaviour and the implication that the sum total of one's acts in a previous life will determine one's present station in this and future lives. A better reincarnation is promised to those whose deeds and actions are good in this station. The ultimate goal is spiritual salvation, or *moksha*, a freeing from the cycle of rebirth.

While this teaching has served to sustain the rigid hierarchy of the caste system, it is not so fatalistic as some would have it. The Hindus say we cannot escape our *karma*, but that with good judgment and foresight we can use it to our advantage.

By the 19th century, reformers such as the Bengali Ram Mohan Roy tried to bring Hinduism into line with imported European ideas, but the monkey-god Hanuman and elephant-headed Ganesh are still idolised, and no one denies the sanctity of the cow and all her products: milk, curd, butter and dung. One of the more notorious practices, self-immolation of widows, known as *sati* (some ultra-traditional castes believe that a widow becomes *sati*, a 'virtuous woman,' by climbing onto her husband's funeral pyre), was outlawed by the British in the 19th century and has now almost disappeared.

Even today, the intricate Hindu caste system can play a role in the Indians' choice of job, spouse and political party, despite the numerous anti-discrimination statutes passed since Independence. Brahmins, the priestly caste, fill many of the top posts in the universities and administration; many Indian Army officers can trace their ancestry to the proud Kshatriya warrior caste; business is dominated by the merchant or Vaishya caste; and Shudras till the land. Casteless Indians, formerly dubbed 'Untouchables' but now

Spots: sacred and secular

With the aid of a small mirror and a graceful arching hand gesture that is consecrated in temple sculpture all over India, pilgrims use white, yellow or red paste to daub a *tilak* – or *tika* – mark on their forehead, which denotes their sect according to whether they are devotees of Vishnu or Shiva.

Women apply red ochre to a parting in their hair to denote their married status. These days many Indian women, whether married or unmarried, wear a spot in the centre of the forehead called a *bindi* in any colour, simply as a cosmetic accessory.

Boys heading to the mosque

known as Dalits, have greater opportunities to rise on the social scale these days, a few of them becoming captains of industry and even, in the case of K.R. Narayan, President of the country.

Most marriages in India are arranged traditionally with carefully negotiated dowries. While ever more matrimonial advertisements in the week-end editions of *The Times of India* and and dating websites mention 'caste no bar', just as many specify the required caste or insist on a 'wheatish-complexioned' bride while touting a university diploma or an American work permit.

Islam

India would be unrecognisable without the influence of **Islam**. The great cities of the north, Delhi especially, have all been shaped to a great degree by their Muslim inhabitants, as has Hyderabad, in the south; and India's most famous monument, the Taj Mahal, was commissioned by Shah Jahan, the Muslim Mughal Emperor. Although Muslim Arab traders had been visiting India since the 7th century, Islam arrived in force in the 12th century. Hindu conversions to Islam were generally made out of hope of social advancement under Muslim rulers rather than by force.

Even after partition of the country in 1947, India has the third-largest Muslim population in the world, after Indonesia and Pakistan. For all Islam's hostility to idolatry, uncompromising mono-theism, and opposition to the caste system, the co-existence between

Islam and Hinduism in South Asia has historically been remarkably peaceful. The two religious cultures have fed off each other, resulting in a uniquely syncretic Indo-Islamic culture. In many areas it is not uncommon for local Hindus to worship at the tomb of a Muslim saint, and for local Muslims to take part in the celebrations of Hindu festivals. Unfortunately this mutual tolerance is continually under threat, as fanatics on both sides target each other's places of worship and engage in indiscriminate acts of violence and killing.

Followers of Islam in India are divided into two primary groups: Sunnis (adherents of the Sunna law expounded by Muhammad's own words and deeds) and Shias (followers of those interpretations proposed by Muhammad's cousin Ali). The five core beliefs and practices of Islam (the so-called 'five pillars') are: that there is no god but Allah, and Muhammad is His Prophet; to pray five times every day; to perform acts of charity; to fast from dawn to dusk throughout the month of Ramadan; and to go on the *Haj*, or pilgrimage to Mecca, at least once during the lifetime of the believer.

Sikhism

The most successful attempt to merge the principles of Hinduism and Islam is that of the **Sikhs** ('disciples'). Nanak, their *guru* (teacher), was born a Hindu in 1469 and reared on the egalitarian principles of Islam. He opposed idolatry and the caste system. From Islam he took the idea of one God, but refused any such specific conception as Allah. He saw God's manifestation, like Hinduism, as being everywhere in the world He created. Nanak was followed by a succession of nine other living gurus. The first five Sikh gurus were all poets, whose work was collected to form the basis of the Sikh holy book, the *Guru Granth Sahib*. The militancy of the Sikhs came

An emperor's gift

Tradition has it that the tolerant Mughal emperor Akbar, having been impressed by the Sikh ethos, granted the daughter of the third Sikh guru the area of land in Amritsar on which the Sikhs built their Golden Temple in 1577.

about only after the execution of Guru Tegh Bahadur, the ninth Sikh guru, by the Mughals. His son, Guru Gobind Singh, founded the Khalsa, a committed and baptised group of men and women. The men took the surname Singh, meaning 'Lion' (though not all Singhs are Sikhs), the women Kaur, 'lioness'. Members of the Khalsa wear a turban and keep the five K's: *kesha* (uncut hair and beard), *kangha* (comb for their hair), *kara* (steel bracelet), *kacha* (soldier's shorts) and *kirpan* (dagger).

Sikhs comprise just 2 percent of the population. With strong martial traditions, they make up a fiercely competent élite in the Indian Army, but they are also skilled farmers at the spearhead of the Green Revolution in the Punjab, where most of them live.

Buddhism

Buddhism was founded over 2,500 years ago in reaction to Brahmanic orthodoxy, but it practically vanished as an organised religion from the Indian scene due to persecution and absorption

The Golden Temple at Amritsar

into the Hindu mainstream. However, it continues to exert influence on India's spiritual and artistic life, and is practised by inhabitants of Himalayan regions such as Sikkim and Ladakh, by millions of Tibetan refugees who have made their home in the subcontinent.

The Buddha's own life explains his teachings, but the truth is buried in both legend and historical fact. He was born

Images of Buddha

The 'Ancient Indian' sculptural schools represented Buddha in the form of a symbol, such as a lotus, a tree, a wheel or a stupa. It was only with the emergence of the Mahayana school, patronised by the Kushan King Kanishka, that he came to be depicted in human form.

Siddhartha Gautama in Lumbini (just across the Nepalese border) around the year 563 BC. His mother, who was queen of the Sakyas, is said to have conceived him after dreaming that a magnificent white elephant holding a lotus flower in his trunk had entered her side. Siddhartha grew up in princely luxury, but when he was taken out one day to the edge of the royal parks, he saw the poor, the sick and the aged. Then he saw a religious beggar who seemed serene, and he realised the path his life must take.

Abandoning his riches, Siddhartha went off into the kingdoms of the Ganga Valley. For six years he begged for his food, learned to meditate, and practised severe self-mortification, but still felt no nearer to understanding life's suffering. Then, aged 35, sitting under a tree at the place now known as Bodh Gaya (south of Patna), he vowed to stay there until his goal was achieved. For 49 days he resisted the demon Mara, and became truly Enlightened; 'the Buddha' as he is called today. He preached his new wisdom at Sarnath (near Varanasi) and gathered ever more disciples. The Buddha himself converted many people. He died at the age of 80 of dysentery in Kushinagar, between Bodh Gaya and his birthplace.

Preaching that suffering came from the pursuit of personal desire, the Buddha had advocated the Middle Way of the Eightfold Path: right views, right resolve, right speech, right conduct, right livelihood, right effort, right recollection and right meditation. Only thus could the enlightenment of Nirvana be achieved. This original doctrine, which regarded the Buddha as an enlightened human being rather than as a god or divine being, was embraced by the Hinayana (Lesser Vehicle) school, and spread to Sri Lanka, Burma, Thailand, Cambodia and Laos. The Mahayana (Great Vehicle) school added the concept of the Bodhisattva (Buddhist saint) as divine saviour, and then became the most dominant form of Buddhism, spreading to China and Japan. Vajrayana (Thunderbolt) Buddhism has much in common with Hindu Tantricism, and is particularly influential in Nepal and Tibet.

A Buddhist temple

Jainism

As old as Buddhism, **Jainism** has made its mark with its concept of *ahimsa* (non-violence) and is much more pacifist than its name, which means 'religion of the conquerors'.

Vardhamana Mahavira was its founder. He was born in 599 BC in Bihar and, like Buddha, was the son of a chief. He, too, abandoned riches to become an ascetic. But Mahavira (the 'Great Hero') pursued self-mortification to the end of his life, stripping off his clothes to take his word from kingdom to kingdom. He died of self-inflicted starvation at the age of 72 in Para, near Rajgir. His followers were later to divide into the *Digambaras* ('sky-clad', ie naked) and the *Svetambaras* ('white-clad') you see today.

The religion, in which Mahavira is seen as the manifestation of 24 *Tirthankaras* (teachers, literally 'crossing makers'), attributes souls to all living creatures, as well as other natural objects. Agriculture was therefore abandoned for its destruction of plant and animal life. The doctrines survive in vegetarianism, with Jain monks and nuns carrying brooms to sweep insects away from where they tread and wearing a gauze veil over their mouth to avoid breathing in flies.

In common with Hinduism and Buddhism, Jains believe in the concepts of *karma* and rebirth. Their aim is to pass through 14 stages of the purification of the soul to gain liberation. This is achieved through right faith, right knowledge and right conduct.

Jainism claims 2 million followers in India, including many businessmen in Gujarat and the Deccan, with a few in Bengal. The Jains' nonviolent religion excludes them from agriculture as a profession, but they dominate the electronics industry in Bangalore, banking in Maharashta and the diamond trade in Gujarat.

Parsis, Jews and Christians

Parsis brought Zoroastrianism from Iran in the 8th century AD, and today form only a minute community in the world of religions, with barely 100,000 living in India, mostly in and around the city of Mumbai. They have been and are still enormously influential in this country's economic life, and sometimes serve as go-betweens in the often difficult relations between Hindus and Muslims, and between India and Pakistan.

Their religion dates as far back as the 7th century BC, when their prophet Zarathustra contrasted his peaceful and sedentary People of Righteousness with the polytheistic nomadic People of Evil. Belief in the *Ahura Mazda*, the Wise Lord, is manifest in the three principles of good thoughts, good words and good deeds.

> **Non-violent protest**
>
> Jainism had considerable influence on Mahatma Gandhi's concept of non-violent direct action; he used its fasting-unto-death as a potent moral and political weapon.

Scarce scavengers

The Parsis' traditional method of corpse disposal on their Towers of Silence is under serious threat. Recent years have seen a drastic reduction in vulture numbers, thought to have been caused by the use of an anti-inflammatory drug in cattle. Vultures also keep the countryside clean by scavenging for carrion, and their ever-dwindling numbers have created problems throughout rural areas of the sub-continent.

The Parsis base their code of ethics on the concept of a constant struggle between the forces of creation – light and good – and those of darkness and evil. Its teachings put great emphasis on the purity of the world's natural elements: fire, earth and water. Fire plays an important part in Parsi rituals. Their places of worship are known as 'fire temples', or Agiaries, and contain a sacred fire, which is never allowed to go out. In order to maintain the purity of the elements, Parsis do not traditionally bury or cremate their dead, but lay them exposed and naked on 'Towers of Silence' *(Dakhma)* for vultures to devour.

India's **Jewish** community is ancient indeed. Some texts claim that the first Jews arrived in India at the time of the Babylonian exile, in 587 BC; others bring them to Cranganur (Kodungallur), on the Malabar coast, in AD 72, about the time that the disciple Thomas is said to have brought his Christian mission to India. The oldest Jewish community still in existence is situated down the coast at Kochi (Cochin), dating back at least to the 4th century AD. Some others, less orthodox, can be found in Mumbai, but most emigrated to Israel when it was founded in 1948.

The earliest **Christians** other than St Thomas were the so-called Nestorian 'heretics' of the Syrian Orthodox Church, also living on the Malabar coast since the first centuries of the Christian era. Modern Indian Christians, some descended from the Syrians, others from those converted by British and Portuguese missionaries, number just under 28 million.

A BRIEF HISTORY

India has always been a melange of peoples. Apart from some pre-Ice Age hominids, the first settlers to arrive in India were Negritos and Proto-Australoids. Migrants of Mediterranean stock from the Middle East and Asia seem to have made up the Dravidians, now found principally in the southern peninsula.

In 7000 BC agriculturalists made their first appearance up in the hills of Baluchistan in the northwest. In the Indus River valley, improved techniques permitted the storage of wheat and barley beyond daily needs, and from around 3000 BC a well-organised society built cities at Harappa, Moenjo Daro and around 400 other sites, creating what is now known as the Indus Valley or 'Harappan' Civilisation.

Harappan craftsmen used bricks of a standard size to build two- or three-storey houses that had sophisticated sewage and water-supply

Harappan cities were built mostly of solid brick

The story of Mahabharata carved into the rock face of a temple at Ellora

systems. Houses stood in blocks on a grid layout defined by intersecting streets. Efficient agriculture underlay this urban way of life; among the Harappan animals was a major Indian contribution to the world's food, the chicken.

Modern archaeology suggests that this civilisation was destroyed by floods, when the Indus River changed course, perhaps due to earthquakes, in about 1700 BC.

The Hindus' ancestors

The Aryans arrived on the scene some 200 years later. Originally from the steppes of Central Asia, they migrated to Mesopotamia and then on to Iran before entering India. These fair-skinned cattle-breeders, who saw the cow as an especially sacred animal, practised agriculture in the Punjab after waging war against the region's original inhabitants.

Early events surrounding the Indo-Aryans can be deduced from the later writings of the *Rigveda* (priestly hymns), *Puranas* (ancient tales of kings and gods) and the epic poems of the *Mahabharata* and *Ramayana*. These provided the basis for Hinduism; also, the epics' heroic battles suggest there was a prolonged struggle for land rights over the fertile plains north and east of modern Delhi, followed by invasions and wars.

If ancient writings give only a romanticised view, they do offer a more precise picture of Indo-Aryan society. Their long wars against the indigenous people established their leaders as kings with a hereditary divinity, which the Brahmins (the priests) exchanged for a privileged position of their own. The caste system was already taking shape. Before the conquests, the Aryans were organised in three classes: warriors, priests and commoners. Then they established four distinct categories known as *varna* (literally, 'colour').

As possessors of magical power associated with ritual sacrifice and sacred utterance, Brahmins were the sole interpreters of the Vedic scriptures. They laid down a social pecking order with themselves in first place, followed by Kshatriyas (warriors), Vaishyas (traders) and Shudras (agriculturalists). This organisation became more elaborate as the division of labour became more complicated, so the growing number of occupational groups were subsequently defined as *jati* (subcastes), often living in separate villages. Each caste would preserve its 'purity' by avoiding intermarriage and not sharing food with other castes. Outside these were the casteless, those of aboriginal descent, who performed the most menial tasks.

By 600 BC, the Indo-Aryans had formed monarchies in the Ganges plain, surrounded by smaller tribes resisting the Brahmanic orthodoxy and its authoritarianism. Within the monarchies, thinkers took to the asceticism that has characterised spiritual life in India. The Brahmins cannily countered this threat by absorbing the new ideas into their teachings. But the tribes were less amenable and so became the breeding ground for two new religions espousing non-violence: Jainism and Buddhism.

While rulers fought for control of the Ganges Valley, new invaders appeared at India's frontiers; Cyrus, emperor of Persia, crossed the Hindu Kush mountains into the Indus Valley in 530 BC.

The *Didarganj Yakshi*, a famous Mauryan statue from Patna

While Brahmin and Persian scholars exchanged ideas, the Indians copied the Persian coin system. Rock inscriptions left by Emperor Darius probably inspired the pillar-edicts of Indian Emperor Asoka in the 3rd century BC.

The spectacular invasion by Alexander the Great of Macedonia in 326 BC ended Persian presence, but apart from opening up trade with Asia Minor and the eastern Mediterranean, the Greeks had no lasting impact on India during the two-year campaign. Alexander's dreams of a huge empire extending eastwards across the Ganges plain were blocked by mutinous troops fed up with upset stomachs, the harsh terrain and the tough Indian military opposition. He returned to Babylon, leaving a few governors on the frontier.

The Mauryan Empire

Meanwhile, in the Ganges Valley, Magadha (modern Bihar) emerged as the dominant kingdom. Its ruler, Chandragupta Maurya (321–297 BC), was also to become the founder of India's first imperial dynasty with Pataliputra (modern Patna), the world's largest city at the time, as its capital.

Chandragupta extended his rule to the northwest with a rigorous campaign against the forces of Seleucus Nikator, one of Alexander's generals who had founded the Seleucid dynasty in Iran. It ended in a marriage alliance with the Greeks, but later Chandragupta turned to more sober thoughts: he converted to Jainism, and finally starved to death at the temple of Sravanabelagola.

His son Bindusara combined his father's ambition with a taste for the good life and philosophy. He expanded the empire as far south as Mysore and stunned the Western world by asking the Seleucid King Antiochus for Greek wine, figs and a sophist. The king was happy to send the wine and figs, but would not, however, consent to Bindusara's last request.

To control land and sea routes to the south, the Mauryas still needed to conquer the eastern kingdom of Kalinga (modern Orissa). The task was left to Bindusara's heir Asoka (269–232 BC), admired by Indians as their greatest ruler, perhaps for his special combination of tough authoritarianism and a high sense of moral righteousness. Asoka began by killing all his rivals before conquering Kalinga in 260 BC. This left 100,000 dead, with even more dying from famine and disease, while 150,000 were taken captive.

Famous inscriptions on rocks and pillars everywhere bore testimony to Asoka's reign. The inscriptions state how 'he of gentle visage and beloved of the gods', as he described himself, was filled with remorse and converted to the non-violent teachings of Buddha. But metaphysical implications seem to have interested him less than enforcing a moral example to unite his far-flung subjects under him in peace and fellowship. To oversee this mass conversion, Asoka turned the Brahmanic concept of *dharma* (righteousness) into an instrument of public policy, enforced by the Officers of Righteousness he had appointed for this purpose. The imperial administration for this undertaking demanded a huge bureaucracy, with superintendents, accountants and clerks overseeing commerce, forestry, armoury, weights and measures,

Asoka's legacy

Asoka holds a special place within the modern state, as his lion-topped pillar is the emblem of the Government of India. In 2001, he was transformed into a heart-throb through the big-budget blockbuster movie, *Asoka*, starring Shah Rukh Khan and Kareena Kapoor.

Buddhist caves at Ajanta

goldsmiths, prostitutes, ships, cows and horses, elephants, chariots and infantry. Southern India remained independent, but Asoka had his hands full with a large empire that now extended as far north as Kashmir and east to Bengal.

In the 50 years that followed Asoka's death, Mauryan power went into decline. Agriculture was not productive enough to finance the empire's expansion. Also, the unwieldy bureaucracy could not keep its loyalties straight, with the too-rapid turnover in rulers vying for Asoka's throne.

Kushan rule

After the break-up of the Mauryan Empire, new invaders appeared on the northwest frontier. The first to arrive were Bactrian Greeks left in the Afghan hills by Alexander's successors. They were welcomed for their erudite ideas on medicine, astronomy and astrology.

Joined by Iranian kings known as Pahlavas, the Greeks were over-run in the 1st century BC by bands of Scythian nomads known as the Shakas. They moved on into the Ganges valley when other nomads, the Yueh-chi from Central Asia, swept across the frontier.

Emerging victorious from the struggles between the Yueh-chi and the Shakas, King Kanishka of the Kushan branch of the Yueh-chi established an empire extending from the northern half of India into Central Asia. This put the Kushans in control of the east–west trade that plied the Silk Road between Rome and Xi'an in China. It was a position from which they derived enormous wealth, and under Kanishka this was ploughed into the development of art and culture. Kanishka was a champion of the Mahayana (Great Vehicle) school of Buddhism, which attributed for the first time a quasi-divinity to Buddha; his active patronage of the arts led to the creation of the first bronze and stone sculptures of Buddha – the Buddha in human form.

Buddhist and Jain merchants prospered from the new Silk Road trade and so were able to finance the magnificently sculpted cave-temples in the Deccan, including those at Ajanta and Ellora; in the northwest, the region of Gandhara (around Peshawar in present-day Pakistan) was transformed into a major monastic centre from which the message of Buddhism was sent out to the world. The arts also flourished in southern India during these early times. Madurai was the lively cultural centre for Dravidian artists: poets, actors, singers, musicians, and also dancers who were the precursors of the Hindu *devadasi* temple dancers.

Gupta glory

The Gupta dynasty, founded by the obscure Bihari landowner Chandra Gupta I, rose to power during the 4th century AD. Marriage alliance and military conquest allowed the Guptas to create an empire stretching from Bengal to the Punjab and from Kashmir to the Deccan.

Samudra Gupta, the warrior of the clan, launched lightning raids through the jungles to snatch the gold of the south. The Guptas also captured the western seaports and their trade with the Arabs. They turned their noses up at trade with the Romans, but China offered many bounties, such as silk, musk and amber, in exchange for India's spices, jewels and perfumes, as well as colourful parakeets for the ladies' boudoirs and monkeys for their cooking pots.

The Gupta Empire began to crumble in the 5th century, with the onslaught of the so-called White Huns. They were not clearly linked to Attila's Huns, but their harsh agenda of exterminating Buddhists does suggest an affinity. The White Huns seized the Punjab, Kashmir and a large portion of the western Ganges plain before being chased out again.

In the 7th century, one strong king, Harshavardhana, reigned for 40 years over northern India, and encouraged Buddhist monks and Brahmin priests to participate in philosophical discussions. Sages developed the strict disciplines of yoga and profound metaphysical speculations of Vedanta.

In southern India, power was shared by the Pallavas in Kanchipuram and the Pandyas and Cholas vying for control of Thanjavur (Tanjore) and the fertile Kaveri Delta. The *bhakti* movement of the Tamils

Bhakti

The *bhakti* movement arose during the 4th to 6th centuries AD in southern India as a response to both Brahmanical Hinduism rooted in the Vedas and the stringent rules of Jainism and Buddhism. Moving away from ritual presided over by temple priests, and positing a personal relationship with the divine as the central religious experience, it proved immensely popular and became the driving force in the wholesale revival of Hinduism in South Asia after a long period of Buddhist dominance. Spread in part though the teachings of wandering singer-saints, its influence has remained intense up to the present-day, with the songs of *bhaktas* such as Mirabai and Tyagaraja continuing to be performed; particularly important is the story of Krisna and Radha who become the divine lovers to whom the devotee bares his or her soul. This powerful devotional tradition found its Islamic counterpart in the Sufis who arrived in around the 10th century AD and the creative tension and blurring of the two traditions formed a uniquely tolerant Indo-Islamic culture.

brought a new warmth to the hitherto rigid Brahmanic ritual of Hinduism. The temples of Mamallapuram were a high point in southern architecture, and it was the Pallavan artists who influenced – and may have helped to build – the temples at Angkor Wat in Cambodia and Borobudur in Java.

Islam comes to India

Arab trade with India had long whetted the appetites of the Muslims; when Indian pirates plundered their ships off the coast of Sindh in 711, it pro-

Jama Masjid in Delhi

voked the governor of Chaldea (now Iraq) to send troops with 6,000 horses and 6,000 camels to conquer the Sindh rajas and offer the alternative of converting to Islam or death. When it was revealed to the governor of Chaldea that Hinduism was in fact a serious religion with too many faithful to treat in this way, another solution had to be found: Hindus, along with Parsis who had fled an earlier Muslim persecution in Persia, were given the privileged status of *dhimmi*, dues-paying non-believers.

For nearly 300 years, Islamic conquest in India was confined to this trading community in Sindh, but in the 10th century, tribesmen from Turkistan, driven west by Chinese expansion, set up a state at Ghazni (in present-day Afghanistan) and began raids across the border to plunder Hindu temples. Sweeping through the Punjab and Gujarat across to the western end of the Ganges valley, Mahmud of Ghazni (997–1030) used these raids more to finance his empire in Persia and Turkistan than to set up a permanent foothold in India. Mahmud smashed the infidels' idols and destroyed their temples as he went, but was nonetheless cultured enough to use the booty to build a library, a museum and a splendid mosque when he got back to Ghazni. If Muslims saw him as a righteous militant and Hindus as a brutal monster, neither denied him the title 'Sword of Islam'. In order to understand his ambiguous image, compare him with Europe's crusaders who went on the rampage at about the same time.

There was no concerted Indian response to the invasions because the various kingdoms were busy with wars of their own. The Rajput warrior clans fought each other for control in what is now Rajasthan, the Kathiawar peninsula, and as far east as Khajuraho. The Turco-Afghan invaders were regarded as a transient phenomenon that would either soon disappear or, just like others before them, be swallowed up by the great subcontinent.

A sultan for Delhi

At the end of the 12th century, the Turks arrived: Sultan Muhammed of Ghur and his Mameluke (slave) General Qutb-ud-din Aybak seized Ghazni in 1173 and invaded India. The Rajputs made a belated alliance

Sculpted frieze at Khajuraho

and fought valiantly from one desert fortress to another, but their elephants could not match their opponents' fast horses and superior crossbows. By 1193, the Turks were masters in Peshawar, Lahore and Delhi. The sultan returned to Ghazni and, leaving Qutb-ud-din in charge, moved east to Bengal, destroying centres of Buddhism such as the University of Nalanda.

After his master's assassination in 1206, Qutb-ud-din proclaimed himself sultan of Delhi, head of India's first Islamic dynasty. The sultanate lasted 320 years, but the new sultan ruled for only four years before dying after a fall from his horse.

Sufi spiritualism

Decades before Islam was imposed on northern India by the swords of invaders, a benign and inclusive form of the faith was introduced by wandering missionary-mystics, known as the Sufis, who renounced materialism and sought to draw close to God through direct spiritual experience. The Sufi legacy continues to be felt in India today, particularly at the shrines of its major saints, where devotional, ecstatic *Qawwali* music is performed each Friday evening.

After the shock of the invasion had passed, the Turks proved to be a shot in the arm for India. The Persian language spoken at court enriched Indian literature and combined with the Sanskrit-based dialects of northern India to create Hindustani. Painting and architecture were infused with life, roads were paved, and, in the 14th century, Delhi was pronounced by the Arab traveller Ibn Battuta to be the most magnificent city in the whole Muslim world.

Conversion to the Islamic faith was seen as a means of advancement, and those Rajputs who didn't take advantage of this offer were able to sharpen their martial skills in constant guerrilla warfare. The Turks adopted the Indian cuisine and costume as well as a modified form of the Hindu caste system. Highest were those of foreign extraction such as Turks, Arabs, Afghans and Persians, known as *ashraf* (that is, 'honourable'). Then came upper-caste converts from Hinduism, the 'clean' castes of both merchants and artisans, and then the 'unclean' scavengers.

It is worth noting that the first – and last – Muslim woman to rule in India was Qutb-ud-din's granddaughter Raziyya. 'Wise, just, and generous,' noted a contemporary Muslim historian, 'but she was not born of the right sex and so all the virtues were worthless.' Three years of her wisdom, justice and generosity were all her political dynasty's opponents could take before she was murdered.

Next came Ala-ud-din Khalji (1296–1316), who forced Mongol invaders back across the Afghan frontier and then moved through the peninsula to its southern tip. But Ala-ud-din's successors, the Tughlaq dynasty, did not assert control of the territory. The south remained dominated by the Hindu kingdom of Vijayanagar for the next 250 years.

The Delhi sultanate under the Tughlaq dynasty could no longer hold its own in the north, and independent Muslim kingdoms began to form in Bengal and the Deccan. The end was hastened by the Mongol Timur. Perceiving that the sultans were a soft target, he cut through Delhi in 1398, slaughtering thousands of Hindus and carrying off thousands more as slaves. He left behind him famine and pestilence. The Turks' Indian empire in splinters, it passed into the hands of the Afghan Lodis.

Down on the Malabar coast, the great Portuguese explorer Vasco da Gama landed in 1498, paving the way for his countrymen to form a settlement further north in Goa a decade or so later. The merchants wanted to divert trade away from the Arabs, fearing the enrichment of the North African Maghreb as a threat to Christian Europe. They first tried offering cloth, wine and necklaces for ivory and gold, but the traders of Calicut were insulted at being taken for fools who could be bought with cheap hooch and glass baubles. The Portuguese turned instead to the harder sell of naval batteries, driving off a trading fleet in the year 1509 in order to control the coast.

With the Portuguese merchant adventurers came Jesuit missionaries, who found the best subjects for their teachings among the low-caste Hindus. Around 1548 Francis Xavier began his mission among the pearl fishermen of the Malabar, before he set sail for Japan. To deal with the small communities of Jews and Nestorian Christian 'heretics', who had settled down on the Malabar coast in the mists of antiquity, the then archbishop of Goa opened a local branch of the dreaded Holy Inquisition.

The great Mughals

The next conquerors of northern India did not come uninvited. The Afghan governors of the Sindh and the Punjab, who were hoping for more autonomy than they had under Sultan Ibrahim Lodi in Delhi, therefore called on Babur the Tiger, king of Kabul.

Babur, descendant of Timur and of Genghis Khan, accepted their welcome but made no promises. His men crushed Sultan Ibrahim's 50,000-strong army with matchlocks and mortars, hitherto unknown in India, at Panipat, north of Delhi.

Miniature depicting Timur, Babur and Humayun

It was the morning of 21 April 1526, the beginning of the empire of the Mughals – the term used for descendants of Babur as distinct from those of Genghis Khan, who are referred to as 'Mongols'. Babur fought resistance from the Rajputs and captured Delhi and Agra, then conquered the Afghan chiefs in 1529. His empire stretched from the Oxus River (Amu Darya) in the west to Bengal in the east, with a southern limit marked by the Rajasthan Desert.

Babur died in 1530. His heir, Humayun, preferred opium and astrology to complex state affairs; he was driven out of India into Persia by the Afghan warlord Sher Shah, who proved

An image of Shah Jahan and Mumtaz Mahal

to be a much more able ruler. In five years, Sher Shah built new roads, created a royal postal service, and set the pattern of Mughal administration that would endure for the next two centuries before dying in battle and leaving the throne to a number of inept successors leading, eventually, to the return of Humayun.

Humayun came back in 1555 with a Persian army to recapture the Punjab, Delhi and Agra, but survived only a year before dying after falling down a flight of stairs (see page 70).

His son, Akbar (1556–1605), was one of India's greatest rulers. Typical of his genius was the new religion he offered his subjects: the Divine Faith (Din-Ilahi), intended to satisfy orthodox Muslims and those who, like himself and the Hindus, appreciated the idea of a semi-divine ruler. Keen to win the allegiance of the Hindus, Akbar abolished most of the discriminatory taxes on non-Muslims, and recruited Rajputs for his army after marrying a daughter of Raja Bharmal of Amber (though he did not flinch at massacring another 8,000 Rajput soldiers).

But despite repeated efforts, Akbar could not extend his empire south. In 1565, the Muslim sultanates of the Deccan had conquered the Hindu empire of Vijayanagar, but they were not going to hand it all to Akbar.

Although illiterate, Akbar demonstrated enormous intellectual curiosity. He preferred Sufi mysticism to orthodox Islam, and held debates with Brahmins, Jain monks, Zoroastrians and Jesuits. The more orthodox Muslims were concerned that Islam was being abandoned, and rebellions sprang up in Bengal, Bihar and the Punjab.

While Akbar was fighting in the Deccan in 1601, his son claimed the throne. Akbar rushed back to reassert his power but died soon after, poisoned, it is rumoured, by his son. The new emperor called himself Jahangir (World Seizer) but once in power he left affairs of state to his wife, Nur Jahan, and her father, Mirza Ghiyath Beg, as he was more interested in writing poetry, drinking a great deal of wine, and taking summer excursions up to Kashmir. Here, rich Persian culture dictated taste in dress, decor, manners and morals, enriched by the Hindu culture of the Rajputs in literature, cuisine and sexuality. If the peasants were squeezed by taxes to pay for the luxury of Mughal court life, it was a boon for the country's artisans: goldsmiths, jewellers and weavers. In such an atmosphere, incidents of highway banditry increased and the district governors shared the rich booty in exchange for a pardon when the bandits were captured.

Jahangir's son Shah Jahan became the biggest spender of all the Mughals. He lavished millions on palaces and mosques, shelling

Harems: the cold facts

The Indian Muslims' system of purdah, which strictly confined women to a life behind a screen in special apartments, derived from the old Persian institution of the harem. No men were allowed in the vicinity and armed security guards inside were all female, except for eunuchs who were placed at the outside doors.

In Akbar's time, women were admitted to the harem as an honour to their families, an imperial favour to some politically useful noble, certainly not always nor even very often for the emperor's sexual pleasure. Though he might have had several hundred wives, very few were his regular companions. The senior wife, mistress of the household, was a person of great influence in the realm, guardian of one of the two imperial seals needed to authorise a new statute, and the emperor's confidante in many of his decisions. The most famous example was Mumtaz, the wife of Shah Jahan enshrined in the Taj Mahal, but Jahangir's wife, Nur Jahan, was much more powerful; she practically ran the whole country.

out at least one million pounds sterling on gold and jewels for his Peacock Throne. Despite this, the imperial treasury allotted only 5,000 rupees a week for the plague and famine victims of 1631. Of several hundred women in the emperor's harem, his only love was the now legendary Mumtaz Mahal ('Jewel of the Palace'), by whom he had 14 children in a period of 17 years. When she died, Shah Jahan built her the most famous memorial a man ever offered to the woman he loved: the Taj Mahal.

Shah Jahan's son was Aurangzeb (1658–1707), who overthrew his father and imprisoned him in the Agra fort for the last years of his life. A pious Muslim, puritanical in both clothes and personal tastes, he banished music from the court and burned the portraits of princes as breaches of the Islamic taboo on graven images. Gone, too, was any notion of religious tolerance. The Sikhs were slaughtered, the Hindu temples in both Varanasi and Mathura were destroyed, and the building of new temples was forbidden. Taxes on non-Muslims were brought back; Hindu merchants were forced to pay double duties on their goods. Aurangzeb streamlined the lax administration of his predecessors, but he almost bankrupted the realm with his campaigns to expand the empire down to the south, and his battles against rebels in the north. The most significant resistance came from Marathas, in today's State of Maharashtra, around Bombay. They were led by Shivaji (1627–80) – bandit, brave military commander and an authentic Hindu folk hero.

Starting out from Pune, Shivaji's Marathas fought off the Deccan sultans at Bijapur and the Mughals at Purandar. Aurangzeb forced him finally to submit, but the humiliating reception he was

Mughal miniatures

The Mughal style of miniature painting came out of a fusion of Persian and native art. Initiated by Humayun, the style flourished under Akbar, who left a library of some 24,000 manuscripts, and his son, Jahangir, who was known for his delight in representations of the natural world. Shah Jahan continued the tradition, but later the artists went to regional courts and painting at the Mughal court declined.

given at court sent him back on the warpath again. Shivaji then had himself crowned king of the Marathas and, to pay his soldiers, plundered the country all the way east to Madras.

The British arrive

Meanwhile, by the middle of the 17th century, Dutch and British armed merchant ships had broken through the Portuguese blockade to set up their East India companies on both coasts. Arriving in 1608, the British took five years to get their foot in the Indian door, at the western port of Surat, north of Bombay. The British East India Company destroyed the Portuguese fleet and took over

Robert Clive

the protection of the Muslim pilgrimage ships to Mecca, but that didn't stop the Portuguese making a gift of Bombay (then a tiny, swamp-ridden trading post) to King Charles II in 1661 as part of the dowry of Catherine of Braganza. The Indians were not consulted.

The Company erected its east-coast installations, or 'factories', in the year 1642 just down the road from the Dutch, at Mandaraz, pronounced 'Madras' by the British. Further north, the British gradually gained the upper hand over their rivals, now including the French, for the Bengali trade that was to create Calcutta.

The Mughal Empire had five rulers in 12 years after Aurangzeb died. Bihar, Bengal and Rajasthan all went their separate ways. The Sikhs reacted violently to persecution, and the Marathas spread to Orissa. In 1739, Nadir Shah of Persia invaded, sacked Delhi and carried off the Mughal Peacock Throne (broken up after his assassination).

Meanwhile, the British clerk-turned-soldier Robert Clive won a long campaign against the French for possession of Madras.

Fearing that the Europeans would start carving up Bengal, the *nawab* (Muslim prince) Siraj-ud-daula set up an attack on the British settlement in Calcutta on the hot day of 20 June 1756. Those who did not flee to sea were thrown into Fort William's prison,

Clive of India

Robert Clive (1725–74) is one the more controversial figures in the history of British India, hailed by some as the founder of the Raj and reviled by others as self-serving proto-imperialist. Despatched to Madras at the age of 18 to work as a lowly 'writer' (merchant) in the East India Company, Clive soon found himself embroiled in clashes with the French and their Indian allies. Clive's exploits during the siege of Arcot, despite his complete lack of military training, led British Prime Minister Pitt the Elder to describe him as a 'heaven-born general'.

Clive's lasting fame rests on his exploits in Bengal. In 1756, Siraj-ud-daula, Nawab of Bengal, seized the fort at Calcutta. British forces, led by Clive, headed north, relieving Calcutta and pursuing the nawab's army inland. The decisive encounter occurred at Plassey in June 1757. Despite its fame, the actual battle was something of a non-event, settled when the nawab's commander-in-chief, Mir Jafar, defected to the British side; in return, he was appointed Siraj-ud-daula's successor.

Elected governor of Bengal, Clive oversaw the rise of British power. After victory at the Battle of Buxar in 1764, the Company was granted the diwan of Bengal, Bihar and Orissa, making Clive the de facto ruler of 30 million people – the effective beginning of British rule in India.

Clive returned to England 1767, where he was honoured with a baronetcy but also faced probing questions about exactly how he had managed to amass a vast personal fortune of at least £300,000. In the end, the constant sniping, illness and Clive's long-term history of depression all took their toll, and in 1774 the architect of British rule in India committed suicide, aged just 49.

known as the Black Hole. It is still being debated whether 123 suffocated and 23 survived or 'only' 43 died, leaving 21 survivors, but however many did perish provided provocation enough for Clive to crush Siraj-ud-daula at the Battle of Plassey. Clive became governor and placed his own nawab on the throne, in exchange for £500,000 for himself and the East India Company. He then annexed about 2,330 sq km (900 sq miles) of land due south

The defeat of the Sultan of Mysore

of Calcutta to provide rents for the British settlement and to guarantee himself an income of £30,000 per year for life. The rise of the British Empire in India had begun.

Installing the Raj

The arrival of Indian merchants, including Jains, Parsis and Jews, turned Bombay, Madras and Calcutta into large cities; while the East India Company discovered a knack for large-scale administration. A more ordered form of exploitation took the place of what Clive called 'fighting, chicanery, intrigues, politics, and Lord knows what'. In return for fixed payments to the emperor, Company officials collected revenue. With a well-paid civil service, Clive's successors – Warren Hastings and Lord Cornwallis – avoided the collectors by padding their salaries with private deals. With the title of governor-general, the new 'viceroys' were responsible to the British government rather than the East India Company. Britain began taking India more seriously. But this new interest had in it the seeds of future discontent. Indians were removed from key positions in the administration by Cornwallis, and it took a long time for them to be readmitted to positions of responsibility.

Clive's example in Calcutta set the pattern for territorial control around the country. In the south, Tipu Sultan of Mysore remained a menace to Madras until Governor-General Arthur Wellesley, the future Duke of Wellington, defeated him. Wellesley then turned on the Marathas, whose clans controlled the puppet Mughal emperor in Delhi and much of central India. A few brilliant victories gained control of Orissa and other territories for Britain, but London decided all that energy would be best directed at Napoleon, and called Wellesley home.

When territory wasn't acquired by conquest – Sindh from Baluchi princes, Punjab and Kashmir from the Sikhs, Maharashtra and Delhi from the Marathas, or Assam from Burma – the British annexed it by so-called Principles of Lapse and Paramountcy: if a ruler died without direct heir, his state 'lapsed' into British hands; if, after repeated warnings, a state was judged guilty of misgovernment, it was simply annexed by the Paramount Power – the British.

Schools and colleges were established. Calcutta became the centre of a vigorous free press and the intellectual capital of India. During 1834, regional rupees of differing value were minted with the portrait of the Mughal emperor. Then a national rupee of unitary value was issued, with the face of the king of England. In the interests of running the empire effectively, the British installed railways, better roads, the telegraph and stamp-post. Indians also saw the other side of the Industrial Revolution as their cotton left for Manchester to come back as cloth cheaper than their own. Men such as Governor-General William Bentinck worked with missionaries and reformers such as Ram Mohan Roy to legislate against the practice of widows becoming *sati* by climbing onto the funeral pyres of their husbands. Other campaigns were launched against female infanticide, slavery and the bands of *Thugis* (devotees of Kali) ranging the countryside.

Although some Indians assimilated the language and behaviour of the British, to most the imperialists were offensively aloof. The Indians had known other conquerors, but at least they had been able to gain a sense of them as human beings. The British Raj, though, remained resolutely separate.

The mutiny at Lucknow

Rebellion and reform

The cause of the Uprising of 1857, or the First War of Independence as it is known to Indians, was symptomatic of British insensitivity. Indian troops were trained to bite the cartridges before loading their rifles, but some were greased with animal fat and the Indians felt they were ingesting either fat from the cow, sacred to the Hindus, or lard from the pig, abomination to the Muslims. As they had suffered slights of either incomprehension or contempt for their religious customs before, they simply could not believe it was not deliberate, and an insurrection broke out at Meerut, 40km (25 miles) north of Delhi.

The cartridge blunder became a pretext for avenging other grievances, with troops rallying around the rulers dispossessed by Lapse or Paramountcy. The rebellious army sepoys then invaded Delhi, Kanpur (Cawnpore) and Lucknow, looting treasuries, breaking open jails, and killing British men, women and children.

The British retaliated with equal savagery against the rebels and against civilians in the country through which the relief columns passed. Finally, after re-taking the hub of the rebellion, Delhi,

A *Punch* cartoon depicting British Prime Minister Disraeli presenting Queen Victoria with the crown of India

they condemned the last of the proud Mughals, Emperor Bahadur Shah, to exile in Burma. Nothing could more aptly epitomise the Mutiny's good and bad results, from an Indian point of view, than the name given to the legislation that was to follow: the 1858 Act for Better Government of India. The British decided to tighten their imperial hold.

The East India Company was replaced by a government with a viceroy answering to a secretary of state for India in London. The bureaucracy was to be streamlined, and the army reorganised to raise the ratio of British to Indians. Indian education was greatly expanded, though less successfully in rural areas where people thought it better to be a good peasant than a bad clerk. Queen Victoria, who in the year 1876 would add the title empress of India to her roll of honour, proclaimed that the Indian Civil Service would be open to 'our subjects of whatever race and creed'. However, not a lot of Indians could afford the trip to Britain to take the examination.

Meanwhile, lawyers were at a premium – litigation had become something of a passion in India and it was ideal training for future politicians – and open political debate flourished, especially in Calcutta where Karl Marx was much appreciated (politics had been clandestine up to now because it was so often fatal to express an opinion on the wrong – that is, losing – side).

Modern industry came to the subcontinent, with Indian entrepreneurs developing their own cotton mills in Bombay, Ahmadabad, Kanpur and Madras. But the new tea plantations were a strictly British affair. Indian agricultural products soon found new markets in Europe when the Suez Canal was opened in 1869.

British economic policies were having a devastating impact on the rural peasants. A series of protracted, severe droughts between 1876 and 1902 sparked off food shortages that were compounded by the viceroys' refusal to cap grain prices. As huge quantities of surplus wheat were exported to England, prices soared and poor farmers died in droves. It is now estimated that between 12 and 40 million Indians perished in the ensuing famines.

In the arts, architecture was often the work of engineers, and huge sculptures were ordered from Victorian Britain rather than from local artists. The bright spot was the Archaeological Survey of 1871 to preserve ancient monuments. British soldiers hunting tigers in the jungle were finding temples and palaces many Indians no longer knew existed.

Fighting for Self-Rule

The Indian National Congress, the country's first political party, held its inaugural meeting in Bombay in 1885. As a group of liberal Hindu and Parsi intellectuals, supported by a few progressive British, it was more national in purpose than in its representation. Lacking connection with the peasants, it was also distrusted by conservative landlords and by most Muslims. The goal of *swaraj* (self-rule), proclaimed in 1906, was seen by a moderate Centre group as government within the British Empire, and by a breakaway revolutionary Left group as complete independence.

After years of subservience to the West, artists returned to India themes in their literature, theatre and music. Indians applauded the decision of Lord Ripon to allow Indian magistrates to try British defendants in criminal cases, but attempts at social reform such as protecting child brides against rape by their husbands were fought by traditionalist Hindus from Calcutta and Pune with cries of 'religion in danger'. Self-assertion reigned again: after years of peace, hostilities broke out between the Hindus and the Muslims.

In Maharashtra, a Hindu nationalist cult grew up around the Maratha leader Shivaji (see page 40) against the British and also the Muslims whom Shivaji had fought all his life. Fundamentalists took to the streets to protest against the Muslim slaughter of cows. There was a movement to convert Muslims and Christians back to the 'national' religion. Muslims tried to purify Islamic practice of the Hindu rituals which had accrued over the years.

The caste system was affected by this new spirit. The low caste and casteless pressed for better treatment, but their cause was not helped by the activism of American missionaries and the Salvation Army, who gave other castes a good excuse to resist 'foreign interference'.

Dynamic Lord Curzon, viceroy from 1899 to 1905, was driven by a lofty imperial vision of the British role in India. His grandiose life in the viceregal residence in Calcutta or palace in Simla was worthy of the Mughal emperors.

Highly active in excavating and restoring old temples and palaces, Curzon also did more than any of his predecessors, adding 9,000km (5,500 miles) of new railway lines, working to modernise farming with an agricultural research institute, and building an irrigation system that would become a model for Asia and Africa. But Curzon also tightened press censorship, restored aristocratic privileges and refused to sanction 'indiscriminate alms giving' in the face of massive famine. The Indians also resented his refusal to consult them, and rioted over an ill-considered partition of Bengal. All of this contributed to civil unrest and calls for independence.

'Divide and rule'

After the uprisings in 1857, communal 'divide and rule' became the watchword for the British in India. For example, through the census they forced people to identify themselves in terms of their religion. This fuelled religious tensions in the subcontinent, which persist to this day.

In 1911, King George V became the first British monarch to visit India. He celebrated the fact by announcing that the capital would be moved from Calcutta to a whole new city to be built in Delhi. The royal architects Edwin Lutyens and Herbert Baker created a monumental New Delhi with triumphal arches, palaces, gigantic government buildings and sweeping avenues radiating from circles (for easy riot control) – the stuff of an empire meant to last forever.

In 1917 self-determination in India seemed nearer when London announced its plan for 'the progressive realization of responsible government in

Lord Curzon

India as an integral part of the (British) Empire.' The British were not letting go, but a new Government of India Act two years later promised Indians real executive power at the head of provincial ministries for education, public works, health and agriculture. The moderate Indians were delighted, the revolutionaries saw it as a foot in the door, while many British officials retired rather than serve under Indian ministers.

Riots over Bengal's partition led to new laws for political trials without jury and also internment without trial. Popular protest in the big cities in 1919 at first took the non-violent form of a *hartal*, an Indian 'strike' called when the soul is shocked by an injustice. This idea came from the new leader Mohandas Karamchand Gandhi, dubbed Mahatma (Great Soul) by the Indian poet Rabindranath Tagore.

Gandhi returned to India in 1915 after working as a lawyer defending the rights of the Indian community in South Africa. The moral strength of his non-violent philosophy was immediately tested in the Punjab, where the *hartal* erupted into riots. In Amritsar, the troops of General Reginald Dyer fired on a prohibited mass meeting, leaving 379 dead and over 1,200 wounded.

Gradualist reform became discredited and civil unrest a feature of everyday life. Declaring that 'cooperation in any form with this satanic government is sinful', Gandhi advocated the boycott of elections and the withdrawal of people from government office. Moderates held on, but the election boycott was 33 percent successful.

Gandhi as a young lawyer

Abandoning European dress for a white cotton *dhoti* (loincloth) and shawl, and drawing spiritual guidance from all the great religions of India, Gandhi became the simple but powerful symbol of India. He supported the so-called 'untouchable' castes, whom he dubbed 'Harijans' (Children of God), and defended the rights of village artisans and peasants, but his non-violent movement could not stop the worsening riots among the religious communities.

Worried by the spread of his civil disobedience movement, the British jailed Gandhi in 1922 for two years. In jail at the same time, for 'incitement to rebellion', was Congress Party member Jawaharlal Nehru, who was British-educated but also a Brahmin intellectual, as his honorary title of Pandit suggested. He was the Mahatma's favourite to lead India to independence.

Independence with Partition

The British began to see India's independence as inevitable; however, only a few seemed to understand the vital role of the country's religious groups. Britain prepared a parliamentary democracy with majority rule, but the majority were Hindus – and Hindus, Muslims and Sikhs had been vying for power for many centuries.

Nehru's Congress Party, largely Hindu with a socialist leadership, wanted a parliamentary democracy. As counterweight, British legislation reserved parliamentary seats for religious minorities, but the Punjab and Bengal had such a complicated mixture of Hindus, Muslims and Sikhs that it was not possible to avoid fights over how separate constituencies were to be formed.

The legislation on reserving seats gave the Muslims the basis for an alternative to an India in which they made up only a quarter of the population: Partition. In 1930, the poet Muhammad Iqbal proposed a separate Muslim homeland in the northwest of India. A small group of Indian Muslims at Cambridge came up with the name Pakistan, using the initials of the Punjab, Afghania (Northwest Frontier Province), Kashmir and Sindh (at the same time producing the word *pak*, meaning 'pure' in Urdu), and adding *stan*, the Persian suffix for the word 'country'. The Muslim campaign for Partition was led by the London-trained Bombay lawyer, Muhammad Ali Jinnah.

Meanwhile, Gandhi vehemently opposed any dismemberment of the country, and tried to keep people united by fasting to uphold the spirit of love, and by focusing on the common adversary: the British. Advocating civil disobedience, he led his famous Salt March to the sea, to scoop up salt and

In the trenches

Without giving up demands for self-determination, India fought at Britain's side in World War I, and more than one German general blinked at Rajput and Sikh princes leading Indian infantry across the trenches of the Western Front.

circumvent the hated British salt tax. This put more than 60,000 in jail.

Against this backdrop of militancy, World War II did not elicit the solidarity of the first. Indians courageously fought alongside British troops, in Burma, the Middle East and Europe, but Gandhi saw the British as a provocation for Japanese invasion and was jailed yet again, for launching a 'Quit India' campaign in 1942. Led by Subhash Chandra Bose (aka Netaji) some anti-British extremists even saw the Japanese as a potential Asian liberator.

With riots growing ever more bloody in Bengal, Bihar and the Punjab, India's last viceroy, Lord Mountbatten, arrived with a mandate to make the British departure as quick and as smooth as possible. Quick it was – six months after his arrival – but not smooth. Midnight, 14–15 August, in the year 1947, was a moment, in the words of Prime Minister Nehru, 'when we step out from the old to the new, when an age ends, and when the soul of a nation, long suppressed, finds utterance'.

Statue of Gandhi leading his Salt March

Nehru got his Independence and Jinnah his Partition – a Pakistan whose eastern Bengali portion was to break away 24 years later to become Bangladesh. Bloodshed began as soon as the Partition boundaries were set. In east (Indian) Punjab, Hindus and Sikhs massacred Muslims; in west (Pakistani) Punjab, the Muslims massacred Sikhs and Hindus. This was followed by a mass exodus of millions from one country to the other, but the convoys often ended in slaughter. Delhi itself was torn apart by communal rampages. The overall death toll during Partition amounted to at least 500,000 people.

> **Churchill's view**
>
> Winston Churchill bitterly opposed Indian independence, and so it was probably as well for India that he was defeated by Attlee's Labour Party in the election of 1945.

Mahatma Gandhi immediately rushed from Calcutta to Delhi to defend Muslims against further slaughter. In January 1948, he fasted for peace in the capital city in order to force the Indian government to pay Pakistan the monies due in the Partition's division of assets. A Hindu fanatic, enraged by what he felt was an excessively fervent defence of Muslim interests, assassinated Gandhi at a prayer meeting on 30 January.

Post-Independence India

Sensitive and sophisticated, Pandit Nehru was also the strongest ruler India had known since the great Mughals and, like them, he created a powerful dynasty. Rejecting his mentor Gandhi's faith in a village-based democracy, Nehru worked to make India a fully industrialised society on the basis of democratic socialism. Established industries had their taxes raised but were not nationalised. Companies that were foreign had to accept Indian financial participation and management.

He appropriated for the state much of the personal fortunes of the princes, but found it harder to curtail the power of landowners who had extensive contacts with the more conservative elements in his Congress Party.

Independence negotiations

Nehru's native Kashmir remained an unresolved problem of Partition. The Muslim majority in the Vale of Kashmir and Gilgit should have made it part of Pakistan, but the greater part of the eastern region around Jammu was Hindu, as was the maharaja, Hari Singh. Backed by Pakistan, Pathan tribesmen invaded Kashmir in 1947 to force the issue, but were soon repulsed by Indian troops flown in when the maharaja hastily acceded to India. Kashmir was divided between both India and Pakistan along the ceasefire line, pending a plebiscite – which has never been held. An invasion by Pakistan in 1965 was aborted and ever since the issue has caused a bitter divide between the two neighbouring states, bringing them into military conflict on four occasions.

Applying the principle of geographical integrity, Nehru regained French Pondicherry by negotiation after Independence, and Portuguese Goa by force in 1961. He was less successful in fighting China over territory on the Tibetan frontier. Egalitarian and agnostic, Nehru passed laws against the injustice of the caste system, child-marriage, and the treatment of women in Hindu households, but century-old customs die hard: before his death in 1964, he asked that his ashes be scattered in the Yamuna River at Delhi and the Ganges at Allahabad, but without ritual. The mourning crowds, though, ignored his last wishes, uttering prayers and crying: 'Panditji has become immortal.'

Coming to power in the year 1966 after the brief ministry of Lal Bahadur Shastri, Indira Gandhi proved strong enough in her own right for people to stop describing her as Nehru's daughter.

In fact, she learned much from him and Gandhi: the knack for negotiating the corridors of power of the one and the ability to create a massive popular appeal of the other. She accelerated industrialisation, in particular the nuclear power industry, including a first atomic explosion in the desert in 1974. Her proudest achievement, though, was the Green Revolution that modernised wheat and rice farming to give India a surplus in food production. Old entrenched conservatism hampered her – often brutal and discriminatory against the poor. Birth-control programmes involving forced sterilisations were devised to check the rocketing population growth.

Indira Gandhi's tough brand of authoritarianism was highlighted during the repressive state of emergency declared in 1975. Describing it as 'disciplined democracy', she ordered mass arrests of opposition leaders who had charged her and her party with malpractice and corruption.

The electorate punished her in 1977 with three years in the wilderness, then brought her back with a huge majority. But her second term was beset with the problems of regional unrest, most notably in Assam in the northeastern region of the country, where local massacres left 3,000 dead, and in the Punjab, where Sikh militants staged violent demonstrations for greater autonomy and even independence. It was her order to the Indian Army in 1984 to attack armed militants who had taken refuge in the Sikhs' sacred Golden Temple in Amritsar, resulting in 800 dead, that led to her assassination in Delhi five months later by two Sikh members of her security guard. Hindus then went on the rampage through Sikh communities, resulting in a further round of communal violence.

Indira Gandhi

Riding a wave of popular sympathy, her son, Rajiv Gandhi, and the Congress Party set out on an aggressive programme of 'modernisation'. In addition to a gas leak at the Union Carbide chemical plant that left thousands dead in Bhopal (see page 145) shortly before Rajiv Gandhi's election to office in 1984, numerous regional conflicts at home and a somewhat schizophrenic foreign policy troubled his term. As a result, he and his party were defeated in the elections of November 1989 by the National Front, composed of five parties including the Hindu nationalist Bharatiya Janata Party (BJP). The National Front attempted to set up a new government first with V.P. Singh and later, in 1991, with S. Chandra Shekhar as prime minister. The Congress Party regained power, however, following Rajiv Gandhi's assassination by a Tamil suicide bomber during election campaigns in 1991. P.V. Narasimha Rao, the new Prime Minister, adopted aggressive economic reforms to combat a looming financial crisis.

The BJP's role in provoking the 1992 demolition by Hindus of a mosque in Ayodhya, and the widespread violence which ensued, caused Prime Minister Rao to ban the BJP. Though this party fell into disfavour for some time, their fundamentalist agenda, shared by members of the extreme right-wing Maharashtran nationalist Shiv Sena Party, increased in popularity in subsequent years. Accusations of corruption among officials in Rao's administration in 1995 also paved the way for a comeback. The BJP eventually defeated Congress in the general elections of May 1996, winning the largest number of seats in Parliament. Represented by Prime Minister Atal Behari Vajpayee, the BJP was forced to back down, however, having failed in efforts to form a coalition government. The United Front, composed of 13 parties supported by Congress, placed H.D. Deve Gowda at the helm.

With the backing of Congress, Prime Minister Gowda ruled until May 1997, when Congress unseated him and appointed Inder Kumal Gujral in his place. Despite the instability of the nation's government at this time, it is remarkable that in the year that India celebrated its 50th Anniversary of Independence, a Dalit (or member of an oppressed caste), K.R. Narayan, was appointed president for the first time.

In early 1998, political volatility necessitated India's first ever midterm parliamentary elections, leading Congress to withdraw support from Prime Minister Gujral and to make Atal Behari Vajpayee of the BJP head of a multi-party coalition government. In May, Vajpayee announced the successful completion of nuclear tests, which, although touted by the Indians as a sign of their sovereignty, has complicated India's relations with its neighbours, not least Pakistan, which successfully tested its own nuclear bomb soon after.

Escalating tension between the world's two newest nuclear powers came to a head in the summer of 1999 when it emerged that Pakistani-backed militants had crossed the Line of Control in disputed Kashmir to shell Indian military positions. A full-scale battle erupted high in the mountains around the town of Kargil, ending in a decisive Indian victory.

The ensuing surge in popularity of Prime Minister Vajpayee swept him and his NDA coalition to a convincing win at the polls in 1999.

But the situation in Indian Kashmir only worsened over the coming year, with frequent massacres, bombings, ambushes and suicide raids aggravating already strained relations between India and Pakistan.

However, it was the storming of the Parliament Building by Islamic militants in December 2001 that ultimately brought the two countries to the brink of all-out war. Only intense US-led diplomacy averted what would have been a catastrophic clash between the million or more men at arms who over the months afterwards lined up along the border.

Deteriorating relations between New Delhi's Hindu-dominated government and Pakistan's Islamic military rulers was mirrored by an increase in communal tension in India itself through 2002. After a train of Hindu pilgrims was allegedly attacked by a Muslim mob in Godhra, Gujarat, killing 38, reprisal rapes, riots and massacres erupted across the state. In the backlash, an estimated 2,000 Muslims were murdered and medieval mosques torn down. Gujarat's right-wing Hindu chief minister, Narendra Modi, rejected accusations that he had masterminded the pogrom, but it was widely reported at the time that his police had repeatedly stood by while massacres of Muslims took place.

Far from cementing the rule of Hindu extremism in India, Godhra and its aftermath seems only to have provoked a swing of support towards more secular government. Political commentators were astonished when, in May 2004, the Congress Party defeated Vajpayee's BJP-led NDA coalition in national elections. Congress leader, Sonia Gandhi – Italian-born widow of the murdered Rajiv Gandhi and heiress apparent to the country's most enduring political dynasty – was asked to form a government, but confounded supporters by refusing to take power. Instead, her finance minister, 71-year-old Manmohan Singh – an Oxford-educated Sikh economist – was sworn in as India's first non-Hindu prime minister.

Modern India: rich and poor

At least until the Mumbai terrorist atrocities of 2008, Manmohan Singh's major achievement was to oversee improving relations

Prime Minister Manmohan Singh with Sonia Gandhi

with Pakistan, and make significant steps towards peace in Kashmir. But diplomatic efforts have been played out against a murderous spate of bombings, launched by assorted Islamic militant groups. Natural disasters too have taken their toll – from the Asian tsunami of December 2004, to a series of catastrophic monsoon floods in 2005, 2007 and 2012, and a massive earthquake on the Kashmir-Pakistan border in 2005. The long-term impact of these disasters fell most heavily on the poorest inhabitants of the affected regions, hundreds of thousands of whom are still struggling to rebuild their lives.

Yet their plight has attracted less attention than the economic boom being enjoyed by India's new urban elite. Fuelled by rapidly expanding infotech and back-office sectors, the country has experienced unprecedented growth rates of between 7 and 10 percent over the past decade. Manufacturing output has soared, and sales of consumer goods such as the Tata Nano – the world's cheapest car – have transformed life for the emerging middle classes of cities like Bengaluru, Hyderabad, Pune and Delhi.

'Out-sourcing' may be the buzzword among the country's affluent middle classes, but the trickle-down of benefits from the boom has yet to be felt by the rural poor who comprise four-fifths of India's inhabitants. With a population of over 1.4 billion, the world's largest democracy remains unable to curb corruption in government and ensure an equitable distribution of its vast resources. Millions still lack access to safe drinking water, adequate nutrition, health care and education, while programmes to build gigantic dams, space rockets and nuclear bombs progress at pace. The quandary facing India's rulers remain how the country can continue to balance demands for security and modernisation with meeting the basic needs of its people.

Just how restless its poor have become was underlined in 2011–2012, when anti-corruption campaigner Ana Hazare staged a series of hunger strikes to lobby for more transparent government in India, galvanizing millions to join the protest. Hundreds of thousands of landless poor also marched on the capital to remind the country's leaders that while the lives of the urban elite continue to improve year on year, the lot of the poor majority in rural India has altered little in decades.

More mass protests erupted in the winter of 2012–2013, reminding the world of the extent to which India also lagged behind international norms when it came to gender equality. The death in January 2013 of a young medical student after she was gang raped on a Delhi bus caused an outcry across the country, mostly from the middle classes. Statistics suggest that one rape is reported every 20 minutes in the capital alone, but less than one percent of cases result in convictions; sexual harassment of women in public places and transport is also systematic.

The tragedy exposed the inadequacy not just of the law and judiciary, but healthcare and other basic services supposedly provided by the state in India. Analysts point to the growing gulf between a corrupt government used to a non-accountable, paternalistic style of politics and the transparency demanded by India's newer voters – a rift which looks set to define India's political landscape over the coming decade.

Historical Landmarks

2500–1600 BC Harappan (Indus Valley) Civilisation.

1500 BC onwards Central Asian Aryans migrate to the Indian subcontinent.

563 BC Birth of Siddhartha Gautama, the Buddha.

326 BC Alexander the Great invades northwestern India.

c.325 BC Chandragupta Maurya founds the Mauryan Empire.

c.260 BC King Asoka converts to Buddhism.

c.1200 Muslim armies conquer northern India; decline of Buddhism.

1206 Delhi sultanate is founded.

1498 Vasco da Gama reaches India.

1526 Babur overthrows Delhi sultanate, establishes Mughal Empire.

1631–48 Emperor Shah Jahan builds Taj Mahal.

1642 East India Co. opens trading station at Madras (Chennai).

1690s East India Co. establishes Calcutta (Kolkata) as its main base.

1756 Nawab of Bengal attacks Calcutta; British Empire in India consolidated.

1857 Indian Mutiny; India comes under direct British rule.

1911 George V announces that the capital will be transferred to Delhi

1920–22 Mahatma Gandhi leads Non-Cooperation campaign.

1947 Independence; partition of subcontinent into India and Pakistan.

1948 Assassination of Mahatma Gandhi.

1965 Pakistan invades Kashmir.

1971 Creation of Bangladesh, with Indian support.

1975–77 Indira Gandhi imposes a state of emergency.

1984 Indira Gandhi is assassinated following attacks on Golden Temple.

1991 Rajiv Gandhi is assassinated.

1999 War with Pakistan-backed forces around Kargil in Indian Kashmir.

2003 Kashmir ceasefire begins a thawing of relations with Pakistan.

2004 Manmohan Singh elected prime minister; tsunami hits east coast.

2006 In Mumbai, 207 rail commuters die in terrorist bomb blasts.

2008 Gunmen attack the main tourist and business area of Mumbai; 172 dead.

2009 Congress party sweeps to victory in general elections.

2011 Mass movement against India's culture of corrupt officialdom emerges.

2013 Demonstrations paralyse Delhi when the victim of a violent rape on a city bus dies from her injuries.

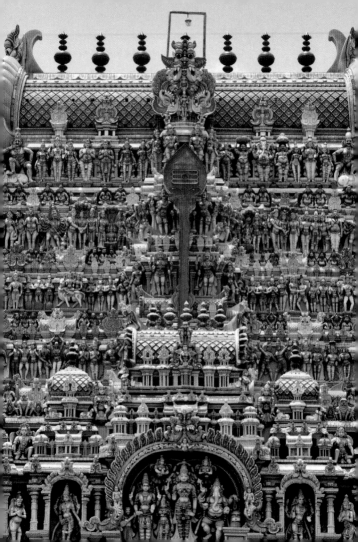

WHERE TO GO

Where, indeed? The subcontinent is so rich and varied that the choice of what to see on a first visit can be daunting. Don't even think of 'doing' India the way people 'do' Europe. With some judicious selection from among the places we suggest, you can most certainly get a pretty good feel for the country in the four weeks that most visitors devote to a first trip.

Even if you have a distinct taste for improvisation and a horror of schedules and detailed itineraries, you must accept from the outset, if your time is at all limited, that travelling around India will demand a certain amount of planning. Remember, there are over one billion Indians out there, and a lot of them will be on the move at the same time as you will be, so you will at least need to make some advance reservations for hotels in principal cities and for your major plane or train journeys. This will still leave you plenty of room for getting off the beaten track and staying overnight in new and unexpected places.

GETTING AROUND

The guide is divided into the following broad sections: Delhi, The North, Rajasthan, The West, The East and The South. It's easy to pick and mix according to time and inclination. Thus, if wanting to follow the classic Golden Triangle route (Delhi, Agra, Jaipur), see the Perfect Tour (see page 4) and refer to the different relevant sections (Delhi, The North and Rajasthan). Those wishing to follow the Ganges plain all the way from west to east will be able to glean their information from both 'The North' and 'The East'. For international visitors the starting points are Delhi for the north, Mumbai for the west, Kolkata for the east and Chennai or Thiruvananthapuram for the south.

The Meenakshi Temple in Madurai

Hitching a ride on a train in Kerala

It's possible to overdose on cultural sights, so a selection of other attractions such as nature reserves and national parks, beach resorts, hill stations, deserts and mountains will be part of most people's itinerary. Even if your budget allows you to fly around the country, you will never be able to cover everything, so it's best to design a 'menu' of places to see in each region.

If you're travelling by train (see page 248) and rate comfort above improvisation, go first class with an Indrail pass. Indrail passes come in three classes, and their main advantage is that they can get you access to 'quotas' when the train is allegedly 'full'. However, travelling with an Indrail pass is a lot more expensive and doesn't always speed up booking.

Flying offers another increasingly viable way of covering long distances with relative ease, thanks to the recent explosion in domestic air services, with a profusion of airlines offering flights to virtually every city of consequence in the country. See page 248 for further details of the relevant airlines. The 'Visit India' scheme run by Jet Airways (www.jetairways.com) offers one- to three-week India-wide air passes, a convenient, if not especially cheap, option.

Tourist information offices can be very helpful. You will find their guides are much more reliable than those outside the temples or palaces, but one word of warning: different tour guides will give contradictory explanations about the significance of statues as well as many different versions of legend and historical 'fact'. It would be easy to dismiss these explanations as being nonsense, but you'll understand India better if you can appreciate that what each guide is saying may in its own way be true.

Practical hints

The climate in India imposes its own imperatives and restrictions on your itinerary. The Himalayan regions are simply impractical in winter, Delhi unbearably hot in June, and flights everywhere uncertain in the monsoon. Think of three seasons – cool, hot and wet – emphasised here because they take on a particular meaning in the Indian context. The cool season is from November to February, the ideal time for seeing most of India (except the northern hills and mountains, where it's bitterly cold). Cool means it is pleasantly warm by day, and fresh enough for a sweater in the evening. The temperature begins to rise by mid-February. Hot, from mid-March to June, is hot as people only rarely experience it. The cities and plains in this season are definitely a bad bet, but the hill stations will be at their best. From mid-June through September, wet means monsoon-wet, not all day every day, but torrential rains occur often enough to make travel uncertain and the mosquitoes

Religious decals on a Kolkata taxi

and other bugs a real nuisance. However, during this time the country is at its most green, and the monuments, especially the Taj Mahal, take on a glistening beauty.

With regard to your health (see page 237), two attitudes almost guarantee a miserable time: carelessness and hypochondria. Take elementary precautions by sticking to bottled drinks and freshly cooked food, and you shouldn't have any serious stomach problems. An occasional touch of 'Delhi belly' is unavoidable when you're not used to the spicy food, but nothing to worry about; take it easy and drink lots of liquids, and it will pass. If you are on a short trip, you may need to take a quick-acting remedy to keep you on your feet, but if you load up with antibiotics and a host of other patent medicines, your body will never build up resistance, and the next attack will just be worse.

It is essential to protect yourself from the heat. Save your suntanning for the beach or the hotel swimming pool. Otherwise, stay out of the sun. Wear a nicely ventilated hat and keep to the shade in the street. Try to do your open-air sightseeing in the morning and late afternoon. Take a siesta after lunch. Drink plenty of liquids – in the heat, dehydration is more of a risk than an upset stomach.

In all senses of the word, stay cool. In the first few days jet-lag, acclimatisation and culture shock may lead you to lose your temper when you see the airports, railways and hotels not organised in a way you're used to, but don't forget that John Kenneth Galbraith called it a functioning anarchy. Count to ten, and, like Delhi belly, it'll pass. Airports, railway stations and hotels can be a pain anywhere in the world these days. Indians are mostly cheerful, responding much more readily to a smile than a scowl.

The red tape can at times seem like barbed wire, but this, too, can be handled. Part of India's legacy after several centuries of bureaucracy (don't just blame the British civil service – it began long before) is an inordinate respect for the written document and the rubber stamp. Don't knock it – use it. Vouchers, passes, letters of introduction and printed business cards all work like magic when a 'confirmed' reservation has become 'unconfirmed'.

Echoing around every office you will hear the cheerful phrase: 'No problem'. Though it rarely means exactly this, interpret it as meaning 'no catastrophe' and have a good time anyway.

DELHI

Situated on the Yamuna (Jumna) River, **Delhi ❶** was repeatedly a target for conquerors from the northwest. They each very often destroyed the work of their predecessors, but the city remains a fascinating compendium of India's imperial history.

Recent archaeological finds suggest that a site on the Yamuna may have been the home of *Mahabharata* hero Yudhishthira, dating back to 1000 BC. A rock inscription from Emperor Asoka indicates that Delhi was a major point on the trade route between the northwest frontier and Bengal in the 3rd century BC.

The Tomara Rajputs made it their capital in AD 736, with the name of Dhillika, and it was a focus of clan wars until the Muslims

A busy street in Old Delhi

The Qutb Minar

conquered it and Qutb-ud-din Aybak set up his Sultanate in 1206. Delhi was dismantled to make way for new monuments, which then suffered from the devastating passage of Timur in 1398. He took away 90 elephant-loads of building materials and thousands of skilled Delhi stone-masons and sculptors to work at his capital in Samarkand. With the advent of the Mughals in 1526, Delhi alternated with Agra as the capital, and each ruler asserted his particular taste in architectural caprice.

Under the British, the town took a back seat to the ports of Calcutta, Bombay and Madras until 1911, when it became once more a proud imperial capital. No less vain than the Mughals, the new conquerors all added to New Delhi their own architectural preferences, which were a tribute to India's past but unmistakably British in overall conception.

It is possible to sign up for guided tours of the capital, which take you through a mixture of imposing ministries and embassies, modern office buildings and hotels, and along the Old Delhi of vibrant Hindu and Muslim communities crowding in on the Mughal monuments. For more information, visit the India Tourism office at 88 Janpath or visit www.delhitourism.nic.in.

Delhi of the sultans

Start at the southern end of the city, with the **Qutb Minar** Ⓐ, a symbol of Islam's impact on India. Begun by Delhi's first sultan, Qutb-ud-din, but not finished until 1368, the 73 metre (240ft) tower was erected to celebrate the sultans' conquest of Delhi. The tower comprises five storeys, each a tapering cylinder with angular and convex ribs, separated by balconies. The top of the tower is off limits, due to dangers inherent in the narrow staircase that leads to the look-out point, so the best bet for a panoramic view of the city is the top floor of one of the taller, more recent hotels.

Adjacent to the Qutb Minar, the ruined **Quwwat-ul-Islam-Masjid** (which means 'The Might of Islam') was built by local Hindu craftsmen as Qutb had no skilled Muslim labour at his disposal. The materials came from 27 Hindu and Jain temples, which had been demolished by the craftsmen's own elephants. You can see the results in the temple-pillars set on top of one another. Sculptures have been plastered over, but the Indian carving remains. Islamic architecture shows in the five characteristic peaked arches of the prayer-hall screen, but even here the decoration is naturalistic and Hindu in style.

In the mosque's courtyard there is a 7 metre (22ft) **Iron Pillar** from the 4th century, brought here by the Rajput founders of Dhillika, but nobody knows from where. Rust-free even after 1,600 years' worth of monsoon, this monument to Garuda, the Hindu god Vishnu's winged vehicle (*vahana*), is said to have special properties.

Victorian vandals

Mongols and Persians were not the only plunderers to vandalise Delhi. Most of the Red Fort's palace apartments were dismantled by the British to build army barracks after recapturing the city from the 'mutineers' in 1857. This officially sanctioned vandalism has to be understood within the context of the vindictive climate that reigned after the mutiny. Some of the more enlightened viceroys did their best to make amends in order to protect and restore India's patrimony. But Lord Curzon and other officials often had to contend with philistine circuit judges, who thought nothing of whitewashing or plastering over frescoes in a Mughal mausoleum while turning it into a rest house.

City of the Mughals

Due east of New Delhi's India Gate, the much-plundered 16th-century Purana Qila (Old Fort) stands on an ancient mound, now believed to mark the site of Indraprastha of the *Mahabharata* epic.

Here, the earliest Mughal building in Delhi, the **Qila-i-Kuhna-Masjid**, with its minutely detailed moulding of graceful peaked arches, represents an important transition from the Turco-Afghan to the sophisticated style of the Persian-influenced Mughals. The mosque was built in the year 1541 by Sher Shah. **Sher-Mandal**, the octagonal tower due south of the mosque, served as Sher Shah's pleasure-palace, but it was to be the death of his rival and successor, Humayun.

From Humayun's death came the splendid monument located in Nizamuddin, **Humayun's Tomb B**, which was built by his widow Haji Begum and was one of the inspirations for the Taj Mahal. It stands on a raised terrace in a set of walled-in, tree-shaded lawns, but without the water once running in its channels ('rivers of life'), or the rectangular pools that were to grace the grounds of the Taj. Humayun's tomb has a remarkable charm of its own, a site for repose and serenity made from a delicate combination of materials – buff-and-red sandstone and smart, grey-trimmed white marble. With a majestic dome uniting the four octagonal kiosks over the terrace's latticed arches, this is the first fully-realised masterpiece of Mughal

Death of an emperor

On 24 January 1556, Humayun was about to descend from the rooftop of the Sher Mandal in the Purana Qila, which he had had converted into a miniature observatory. At the top of steps, he heard the *muezzin* launch into the call to prayer from the nearby mosque. Turning to bow, the emperor tripped, fell and struck his head on the hard stone steps below. He died three days later. Humayun thus, in the words of one historian, 'stumbled out of his life as he had stumbled through it,' an unfortunate end to the life of the unluckiest of all the great Mughals.

Keeping the Lal Qila spic and span

architecture. The numerous six-pointed stars set in the abutments of the main arches are not the Jewish Star of David but an esoteric emblem that you will see all over the country.

Red Fort

Dominating Old Delhi, the **Lal Qila** ⊙ (Red Fort) was built by Shah Jahan when he transferred the capital back to Delhi from Agra, and was completed by 1648. Behind its ramparts, the Delhi citadel is more a palace than a fortress, with white marble preferred over the region's red sandstone. It is thought he used the same architect who worked on the Taj Mahal.

From south of the fort, notice the two monumental elephants outside the Delhi Gate. Part of the original design, they were destroyed by Emperor Aurangzeb, who considered such images idolatrous. Viceroy Lord Curzon had these replicas installed in 1903. Enter the fort on its west side at the Lahore Gate and you'll find yourself in a vaulted bazaar street, an idea Shah Jahan borrowed from Baghdad. Imagine Rajput princes riding on elephants through the arcade as far as the **Naubat Khana** (Drum House), where the imperial band played and visitors were obliged to dismount.

Pass with the ghosts of these nobles and commoners through the Drum House to the **Diwan-i-Am** (Hall of Public Audience). Here, under a baldaquin with 40 pillars, the emperor sat cross-legged on his throne, the 'Seat of the Shadow of God'. He held audience, surrounded by nobles, at midday, while common petitioners attended in the courtyard below. As a visitor, you can admire the inlaid stone panels of birds and flowers at the back of the hall.

Entrance to the **Diwan-i-Khas** (Hall of Private Audience) was for the privileged, by ticket only. You will find it on the left, among the palace apartments on the Yamuna River. Beautiful as it is, with carved designs on the marble columns and cusped arches, imagine it in its full glory before the ravages of Nadir Shah in 1739. His Persian troops chipped the gold out of its pillars and inlay off the ceiling, and then carted away the fabulous Peacock Throne. Above the arches you will see the inscription:

If paradise on earth there be,
'Tis here, 'tis here, 'tis here!'

Worse damage still was inflicted to the fort by the British, after they re-took it from Bahadur Shah's poorly organised defenders at the end of the 1857 uprising. Whole wings of exquisitely carved palaces were levelled and ugly brick barracks erected in their place. One of the few surviving apartments is the principal harem, **Rang Mahal** (Palace of Colour). The walls' paintings have gone and water no longer flows in its indoor Nahr-i-Bihisht (River of Paradise), but mosaics made of mirrors ornament the ceiling and walls of six boudoirs, making a galaxy of stars when candle-lit. Southernmost of the palace buildings, **Mumtaz Mahal** was part of the imperial harem and is now a small museum of Mughal artwork.

To the northwest of the Diwan-i-Khas, the **Moti Masjid** (Pearl Mosque) is the one contribution to the fort by Shah Jahan's successor, Aurangzeb. Each evening, a sound and light show at the Red Fort tells its story; details can be obtained from the India Tourism office at 88 Janpath.

Chandni Chowk, the road from the Lahore Gate, was once a processional avenue. Today, it is the main thoroughfare linking Old Delhi's bazaars selling jewellery, clothes and traditional sweetmeats.

Mahatma's memorial

The **Raj Ghat**, the simple memorial to Mahatma Gandhi overlooking the Yamuna River, is far in spirit from the Mughals but an integral part of Old Delhi. On lawns planted with trees donated by visiting heads of state, a square of marble marks the place where Gandhi was cremated. The platform has an inscription recording his last words – Hé Ram (Oh, God) – and nearby, a sign declares that most famous Gandhi talisman: 'Recall the face of the poorest and most helpless man whom you may have seen and ask yourself if the step you contemplate is going to be of any help to him.' There is also a museum recording the highlights of Gandhi's life. To the north is **Shanti Vana**, where members of the Nehru dynasty have been cremated.

Gandhi memorial at the Raj Ghat

On an outcrop of rock southwest of the Red Fort stands Shah Jahan's other great construction, the **Jama Masjid**  (the great congregational 'Friday Mosque'). The inadvisability of a morning or late afternoon visit on hot days will become apparent when you see the three pyramidal flights of stairs to the gate-houses. The 100 sq metre (1,076 sq ft) courtyard is enclosed by long colonnades with a pavilion at each corner. The prayer hall highlights the emperor's aesthetic, in the lotus calyx on the gateway's two lantern shafts, the delicately flaring balconies on the minarets, and the stripes to emphasise the bulbous marble domes.

New Delhi

Those nostalgic for the British empire please note: Clive Road has been named Tyagaraja, Queen Victoria Road has become Rajendra Prasad, and Curzon Road is Kasturba Gandhi Marg. Though the statues of British leaders have also disappeared, the British spirit remains in the city's planning. Faithful to the policy

The Jantar Mantar was built in 1724

of separating the British cantonment from the Indian quarters with a railway as the barrier, the new city built for the empire's Indian seat of government is separated from Old Delhi by the line running from Amritsar to Agra. British neoclassical architecture here is mixed with elements of the Buddhist, Hindu and Mughal past, and the geometry of its plan exudes the self-confidence of the empire. As a visiting statesman once said of it: 'What splendid ruins it will make!'

The commercial hub of New Delhi is the circular arcade and bustling roundabout of **Connaught Place** Ⓔ. With cinemas, banks, travel agencies, restaurants and craft emporiums, it's one place whose new name, Indira Chowk, does not seem to have caught on.

The **Jantar Mantar**, set south of Connaught Place, is perhaps the strangest monument in New Delhi. It is difficult to believe that its bizarre shapes, staircases going nowhere and windows in walls without rooms were built in 1724 by a serious student, rather than in the last century by some deranged architect. It is in fact the astrologico – that is, the astronomical observatory – of Rajput King Jai Singh II from Jaipur. Its centrepiece is the right-angled triangle, Samrat Yantra (the Supreme Instrument), with a dome acting as a sundial, 'accurate to half a second.' In addition to this structure, he built four more – in Ujjain, Varanasi, Mathura and his native Jaipur.

Near the Jantar Mantar, you can witness the joyous atmosphere of popular Hinduism at the **Hanuman Mandir** (aka the 'Monkey Temple'). Hanuman is a beneficent deity predating classical Hinduism, and the reason why no one would dream of harming the little langurs and macaques running around here.

Connaught Place straddles the northeast–southwest axis that links the Jama Masjid mosque of Old Delhi to India's parliament, **Sansad Bhavan**. Designed by the famous Herbert Baker, the rather too massive, colonnaded rotunda of the parliament building is at its best illuminated at night.

The Viceroy's Residence, now the President's house, **Rashtrapati Bhavan**, has wings radiating from the great grey-blue dome of the central block and the tranquil pools and lawns of its gardens, and so bespeaks the grandeur of Britain's heyday. It looms from an artificial hill along the processional avenue, **Rajpath**  (once Kingsway), which is flanked by parklands, where India holds its marches on Republic Day, 26 January. At the other end of Rajpath stands **India Gate**, the war memorial designed by Edwin Lutyens in the style of a triumphal arch that pays tribute to 90,000 Indian Army soldiers who died in World War I. Close by the arch is a cupola that now stands empty. This once held a giant white marble statue of the British King George V, which has been transferred to the site of the coronation durbar in the far north of the city.

Delhi's museums

The **National Museum** , on Janpath (Queensway) just south of Rajpath, contains a matchless collection of antiques spanning 5,000 years of Indian history, gathered from across the subcontinent. Allow at least three hours to do it justice.

India Gate at dusk

Railway buffs will enjoy the display of early steam engines at the open-air **National Rail Museum**. It is situated in the diplomatic neighbourhood of Chanakyapuri, southwest of Rajpath.

The **Nehru Memorial Museum** is devoted to Independence and the life of India's first prime minister. It is located in the house that Nehru inherited from the British Indian Army commander-in-chief on Teen Murti Road (it also houses a planetarium).

THE NORTH

This section encompasses the states of Uttar Pradesh, Punjab, Himachal Pradesh, Jammu and Kashmir, and Uttaranchal. The heart of the Mughal empire can be found at Agra, with the incomparable Taj Mahal, as well as the nearby abandoned city of Fatehpur Sikri. The holy city of Varanasi is the very soul of India, while memories of the Uprising are kept alive at Lucknow. Punjab is home to the Sikh city of Amritsar with its extraordinary Golden Temple. In the Himalayas there is the hill station of Simla and the glorious Kullu Valley; there's also Ladakh, with its Buddhist monasteries, lying beyond the passes to the north; and the Garhwal, home to Hindu holy sites such as Gangotri. And beneath all that, is the magical Corbett National Park.

Agra

Location of the Taj Mahal, **Agra ❷** is the most popular tourist destination in India. Even if the place had nothing else, it would be worth the trip, for the Taj, as one calls it, is a 'sight' that awakens the wonder and enthusiasm of the most blasé, world-weary traveller; a sight for which no amount of stunning photography in guidebooks and magazines can adequately prepare you.

But there's plenty more. Agra was the capital of Akbar the Great, the site of his fort, of his tomb outside the city at Sikandra, and, several kilometres west at Fatehpur Sikri, of the marvellous deserted town he built to celebrate the birth of a son and which he abandoned to fight on the northwest frontier. Descendants of the

Sunrise at the Taj Mahal

craftsmen originally brought here continue a tradition in jewellery, brassware, ivory and inlaid marble.

The first historical mention of Agra is in 1501, when Sultan Sikandar Lodi made it his capital. Babur captured it along with the Koh-i-Nur diamond, now among the British crown jewels. His grandson Akbar chose Agra for his capital over Delhi.

In the 17th century, Jahangir made it a major focus of the Islamic world. His son Shah Jahan lost his taste for Agra after finishing the Taj Mahal for his wife Mumtaz Mahal following her death. He moved the capital back to Delhi again in 1648, leaving the city's treasure to vandals (including the British) after the 1857 'Mutiny', until the viceroys organised its restoration. Today it is the effects of pollution that are taking their toll on Agra's monuments.

Taj Mahal

This is truly a monument for all seasons. There are those who swear by the sight of the **Taj Mahal** in the Sharad Purnima, the first full moon after the monsoons, a cloudless midnight in October when the light is at its clearest and most romantic. Others love to see it in the middle of the heaviest monsoon, its marble translucent, its image blurred in the rain-stippled water channels of its gardens. But its magic is strong at any time of year, and any moment of the day. At dawn, its colour changes from milk to silver to rose-pink, and at sunset it is golden. Observe it, too, in the brilliance of midday, for then it is utterly, dazzlingly white.

The **gateway** to the gardens of the mausoleum can be admired as a masterpiece in its own right, with graceful marble arches, the domed kiosks on the four corner turrets, and two rows of 11 small *chattri* (umbrella-domes) just above the entrance. It provides visitors with the perfect frame for a first view of the ensemble.

The *char bagh* (foursquare) gardens are an integral part of the Taj Mahal, both spiritually, as the symbol of the Paradise to which Mumtaz Mahal has ascended, and artistically, to enhance the colour and texture of the mausoleum. The dark cypresses heighten the brilliance of the monument's marble, and the water channels (on those rare occasions when they're full), meeting at a broad central viewing platform, not only provide a perfect second image, but also, with the reflection of the sky, add at dawn and sunset a subtle illumination from below.

Exquisite harmony and refined symmetry are the keynotes of the mausoleum itself. The structure is clad in miraculously white marble from the Rajasthan quarries of Makrana, achieving a magnificent texture with the subtly alternating broad and narrow slabs. Standing protectively at the four corners of the raised terrace, the minarets are, deferentially, slightly lower than the sublime central cupola. Inside, the octagonal cenotaph-chamber contains the ceremonial marble coffins of Mumtaz Mahal and Shah Jahan, while muted snatches of daylight

Taj tips

Don't try to do Agra in one day. It is possible (and certainly better than missing it entirely), but it means you won't see much more than the Taj and, say, the fort. More important, you might miss the unique beauty of the Taj as it changes in the light of different times of day.

filter in through the beautiful marble trellis screens (*jalis*). As was the custom of that time, the actual bodies are entombed in another chamber directly below.

Sadly, vandals removed all of the tomb's treasures, but they did leave the gentle beauty of roses and poppies in rich inlaid stones of onyx, green chrysolite, carnelian and variegated agate. The mausoleum is flanked by two almost identical red buildings, to the west a mosque and to the east a building that may have served as a guest pavilion, though its principal purpose was to complete the symmetry of the architectural composition. Each is a perfect viewpoint: try the pavilion at sunrise and the mosque at sunset. But go around the back of the Taj, too, to the terrace that overlooks the Yamuna River. This boasts a view as far as Agra Fort. At dawn, one of the best (and cheaper) viewpoints is from the opposite bank of the river, where, as archeologists have recently discovered, Shah Jahan planned a mirror image Taj made of jet-black marble. Boatmen line up to ferry visitors across.

A marble requiem

Mahal means palace, but in this case Taj Mahal is a diminutive of the name Mumtaz Mahal (Jewel of the Palace) which Shah Jahan's cousin was given when she married him. Daughter of his mother's brother, she had been his constant companion long before he succeeded to the throne and was later first lady among the hundreds in his harem. In 19 years of marriage, she bore him 14 children, dying with the birth of the last in 1631.

Legend has it that Shah Jahan's beard – he was 39, one year older than his wife – turned white practically overnight when she died, and he continued to mourn for years, dressing in white on each anniversary of her death. The 12 years taken to build her mausoleum, working untiringly with his Persian architect and with craftsmen brought from Baghdad, Italy and France, may be regarded as the supreme sublimation of his grief. 'Empire has no sweetness for me now', he wrote. 'Life itself has lost all relish.'

Agra Fort

Built by Akbar in 1565, during a more embattled period than that when Shah Jahan constructed the Red Fort in Delhi, **Agra Fort** was conceived as a citadel with a moat on three sides and a river on the fourth. Pleasure palaces were a secondary consideration, and were in fact mostly added by Shah Jahan.

The entrance from the south, at Amar Singh Gate, takes you up a ridged elephant's ramp, sloped to slow down any potential attackers. Pass into the long quadrangle of the pillared **Diwan-i-Am** (Hall of Public Audience). It was here that Captain William Hawkins handed Emperor Jahangir a special letter of introduction from King James I. Due

The Amar Singh Pol gate at Agra Fort

north you'll see the marble domes of Shah Jahan's **Moti Masjid** (Pearl Mosque), though sadly this is currently off limits to visitors.

Just off the northeast corner of the Diwan-i-Am, the harem had its very own mosque, **Nagina Masjid**; a Hindu temple, the **Mandir Raja Ratan** (built in 1768 during the Jat occupation); and between the two a bazaar where merchants sold silks and jewels. Near the hammam (baths), the **Diwan-i-Khas** (Hall of Private Audience) has rich carving and inlaid marble. The crack in the marble throne came from a British cannonball in 1857. As in Delhi's fort, most of the private palace apartments face the Yamuna River. Among the most charming are the arcaded loggia and the gilt-roofed pavilions of the **Khas Mahal** (Private Palace). A minute staircase led to the **Musamman Burj**, the pavilion of the emperor's chief wife. It is also popularly

The tomb of Itmad-ud-Daulah

known as the 'Prisoner's Tower' for Aurangzeb imprisoned his father Shah Jahan here, allowing him a view of his beloved Taj Mahal.

The **Palace of Jahangir** is built around a square court with arches. There are Hindu motifs on the ceiling in the main hall, and in one on the western side: peacocks holding snakes in their beaks, for example.

On the river bank opposite Agra fort is the **Tomb of Itmad-ud-Daulah**, overshadowed by the Taj Mahal but still of exceptional beauty in its own right. The mausoleum was built 15 years earlier by Jahangir's wife, Nur Jahan, for her father, who served as Mughal *wazir* (prime minister). There's a fragile elegance to the white marble pavilion's silhouette, with a cupola and four octagonal turrets, topped by domed kiosks. The fine lattice-work on the arches and windows is superb, but its outstanding feature is the marble inlay, which is even more abundant than in the Taj, and better preserved.

Fatehpur Sikri

In a country of crowded cities, it makes a refreshing change to travel 37km (22 miles) southwest of Agra to the outcrop on which stands the citadel of **Fatehpur Sikri**, briefly Akbar's imperial capital.

Fatehpur, planned as a capital with Agra as a fallback position in case of attack, is protected on three sides by ramparts measuring about 6km (4 miles). On the fourth side is an artificial lake stretching 8km (5 miles) to the Rajasthan border, never sufficient, apparently, for the needs of the citadel, and so one of the probable reasons why Akbar did not settle here permanently (the explanation most often advanced is that its water supply was inadequate and polluted with salt). Built by the architects working on the Agra Fort, the citadel adds the darker red stone of the mountain ridge to the usual pink sandstone of this area.

Entering via the **Agra Gate**, at the northeast corner, one passes on the right the *karkhanas* (workshops) where carpenters, weavers and stonemasons worked.

In the **Diwan-i-Am**, the courtyard used for public audiences, Akbar dispensed his justice while attended by an executioner with instruments of torture and death. The sight of the two of them was felt to be an effective means of getting at the truth. At the foot of the colonnade is a big stone tethering-ring for an elephant whose job it was to crush condemned criminals to death.

Go through the pavilion to the **Daulat Khana** (Abode of Fortune) on the south side of the courtyard, a palace of which the most striking feature is the Hindu nature of its decoration: carved pedestals with stylised elephant heads as capitals and sculpted stone screens.

In the southeast corner of the courtyard is the **Turkish Sultana's House**, or Hujra-i-Anup Talao (the Chamber of the Peerless Pool);

Taj Heritage Corridor

The land along the river separating Agra's two monuments has been at the centre of a massive controversy over the past decade. In 2003, the then Chief Minister of Uttar Pradesh, Mayawati, initiated a large-scale project to clear and re-develop the strip. Dubbed the 'Taj Heritage Corridor', the development cost an estimated $44million, but stalled before completion when Mayawati was accused of embezzling the lion's share of the money earmarked for the scheme – charges of which she was later exonerated by India's Supreme Court. Concrete scars and a few unsightly foundations stand as monuments to the ill-fated project.

The Panch Mahal in the abandoned city of Fatehpur Sikri

animals covering every wall, panel and pillar create the illusion of woodwork rather than stone. Fatehpur is the subject of many colourful stories in which it is impossible to establish a historian's 'truth'. For instance, in the centre of the courtyard is the **Pachisi Court**, a huge chessboard for the game of *pachisi*, where Akbar and his friends are said to have used human 'pieces' – each player using a team of four slave girls in different costumes.

Also, Akbar is said to have come to the **Astrologer's Pavilion**, in the northwest corner of the court, for a daily dose of forecasts from the house-esoteric. The emperor is known to have consulted a whole panel of experts from Hindu and Muslim schools of astrology. Just behind this is the **Treasury Pavilion**, where you can imagine Akbar seated on cushions under the arches and counting the imperial money. The pavilion was known as Ankh Michauli (Blind Man's Buff), because it was where Akbar was thought to have played 'hide-and-seek' with his wives.

The purpose of the **Diwan-i-Khas** is hotly disputed: it is not necessarily the hall of private audience that its name implies.

Dominated by a great central pillar supporting bridges to a balcony, some claim it was here that Akbar held his famous debates with Jesuits, Brahmins, Parsis, Sufi mystics, and Jain and Buddhist monks – the sages arguing while Akbar sat listening atop his pillar, or striding majestically around the bridges and balcony hurling his questions at his listeners. Others insist that it was just a storehouse for jewels. Truth here, even more than beauty, is in the eye of the beholder.

Walk across the courtyard to the beautiful five-tiered **Panch Mahal**, a palace with the Persian system of ventilation known as *badgir* (wind tower): without walls on three sides, it is open for the breezes to sweep in. Each floor is supported on columns diminishing from 84 at ground level to four on the roof. Notice that no two columns on the ground floor are alike. Be careful on the steep climb to the top, but you will find it is well worth it for the wonderful view across the citadel, particularly the palaces of the imperial harem to the southwest. It is thought that Akbar used to entertain his consorts in the topmost pavilion.

The harem's principal residence is **Jodha Bhai's Palace** – built for Akbar's Hindu wife, the first royal spouse not required to convert to her husband's Islamic faith – and was Akbar's favourite residence at Fatehpur. It has one side screening out the summer heat while the other is open to the cooler breezes. Its most cherished feature is the turquoise ceramic tiled roof in the north and south wings.

Fatehpur's **Jama Masjid** (the Friday Mosque), at the south end of the citadel up on

Akbar's mausoleum

Akbar's mausoleum is located at Sikandra, 10km (6 miles) north of Agra. Although lacking the grandeur of the Taj, the tomb complex presents an arresting spectacle, its huge south gate surmounted by four tapering minarets. Inside, the grounds surrounding the mausoleum itself are filled with grazing black buck and troupes of tame langur monkeys. On the cenotaph are the 99 names of Allah.

its mountain ridge, was the very first of the open courtyard-style mosques that became characteristic of all Mughal cities. Notice the carved central mihrab (the recess marking the direction of Mecca). However, the jewel of the red stone courtyard is the marble-clad **Tomb of Shaikh Salim Chishti**. Its facade features black calligraphy; in the cenotaph-chamber there are pretty painted flowers. Originally a more simple monument, its white marble 'skin' was the addition of a very grateful Jahangir who, without the mystic Shaikh Salim Chishti, might never have seen the light of day (see page 86).

Flanking the southern side of the complex, the mighty **Buland Darwaza** (Great Gate) forms an appropriately grand entry and exit point for the imperial city. It was erected in 1576 to celebrate Akbar's triumphant conquest of Gujarat and rises to a height of 54 metres (177ft). Visible for kilometres, an inscription from the Koran is carved over the archway. It reads:

City of victory

The rise and fall of Fatehpur Sikri is the perfect illustration of Akbar's impulsive personality. At the end of 1568, the emperor was 26 and still without a male heir. At Sikri he met a Sufi mystic, Shaikh Salim Chishti, who promised him, given the proper spiritual dedication, not one, but three sons.

'In return for your friendship and grace', said the emperor, 'I'll protect and preserve you.'

Unmoved, the Sufi replied: 'You can name your first son after me.'

The following August, a boy was born. He was duly named Salim (later Jahangir). Overjoyed, Akbar decided to move his capital to Sikri, then embarked on a successful military campaign and came back to add the name of Fatehpur (City of Victory). By 1581 he had abandoned Fatehpur. Only the family of Shaikh Salim Chishti remained, near the shrine Akbar had built for them. Today, 16 generations later, they are still here, but there is no sign of Akbar's people.

The tomb of Shaikh Salim Chishti, Fatehpur Sikri

Said Jesus son of Mary ('Peace Be Upon Him'): the world is but a bridge. Pass over without building houses on it. He who hopes for one hour hopes for eternity; the world is an hour – spend it in prayer for the rest is unseen.

Lucknow

As a logical stopover on your way to Varanasi (coming from Delhi), **Lucknow** is worth a visit for its special place in the history of India's determined fight for Independence – a focus of the Uprising of 1857. It also holds some extraordinary buildings dating from the era when it was the capital of an opulent, refined Muslim dynasty – the kingdom of Avadh, or Oudh.

The site of a bloody siege in which more than 3,000 Europeans (among them 1,400 non-combatants) held out for five months against an army of mutinous sepoys, the **British Residency** – today preserved as a monument – initially commemorated British resistance, but since Independence it has been visited by Indians interested in this relic of their own struggle for self-rule.

On a lawn surrounded by 24 palm trees, a cenotaph pays tribute to Chief Commissioner Sir Henry Lawrence, who was killed during the attack. An obelisk here honours 'Native Officers and Sepoys, who died… nobly performing their duty'. Indians comprised half the 1,700 troops defending the Residency. A little museum inside illustrates the history of the siege, with a model of the first Residency as well as rusty cannons and cannonballs, and prints, photos and letters.

Down by the river, a short walk away, is the **Martyrs' Memorial**, inaugurated in 1957 on the centenary of the Uprising to honour those who fought for India's independence.

Lucknow, with its 18th- and 19th-century mosques, used to be a Muslim stronghold; although the size of its community has now dwindled to only 30 percent of the city's population, it is one of the two most important Indian centres of Shia doctrine, the other being Mumbai. Of the crumbling monuments that remain from this final flowering of high Muslim culture in India, the **Bara Imambara** and nearby **Hussainabad Imambara** are the grandest – fairytale palaces of onion-domes, graceful arches and minarets. Their exuberant architecture testifies to the considerable decadence and refinement for which the Nawabs of Avadh are chiefly remembered.

The Diwan-i-Khas at Fatehpur Sikri

Sadly, both are in a parlous state of disrepair, as is the fine **Daula Mosque** (next to the Bara Imambara) and the towering **Rumi Darwaza** archway (west of the main gates).

On the eastern side of Lucknow in the district of Hazratganj, you can also visit the flamboyant **Shah Najaf Imambara**, whose delightful interior harbours the tomb of

The Imambaras at Lucknow

Ghazi-udin-Haidar. Nearby stands one of India's most famous public school, **La Martinière**, started by a French adventurer in 1761. Its appearance, traditions and curriculum have altered little since the departure of the British.

On the opposite side of the river from La Martinière sprawls a monument to the unbridled madness of modern Indian politics. A vast complex of sandstone ramparts, gardens, canals, walkways and statues extending over 21 hectares (53 acres), the Dr Ambedkar Memorial was built between 2007 and 2009 by the former Chief Minister of Uttar Pradesh, Mayawati – a controversial figure who has provoked as much criticism as praise for her rags to riches rise from one of the most disadvantaged castes. Mayawati spent a straggering $127.7 million on the memorial to the iconic Dalit liberation campaigner, B.R. Ambedkar – in a state where tens of millions of people remain malnourished and without access to clean drinking water. She was subsequently accused of pocketing a portion of the budget, though these allegations have yet to be proven in court.

Varanasi

One thing is certain: you cannot begin to fathom the mystery of India without a visit to **Varanasi** ❸. Not that this old city will 'explain' everything – in fact, its dramatic confrontations of life and death on the Ganges River, and of scholarship and superstition, may only mystify you even further – but the city's aura of sanctity is so overwhelming that it supersedes any need for rational explanations. Perhaps the Muslim conquerors once perceived the Hindus' reverence for Varanasi as a threat – there is no temple in this 3,000-year-old city dating from before the 18th century – but later it became a holy city for Muslims, too, with Emperor Aurangzeb even trying to rename it Muhammadabad.

The name Varanasi, misheard by Europeans as Benares, is derived from its site between the tributaries of the life-giving holy Ganges, the Varuna and the Asi rivers. The god Shiva is said to have poured the river down on the plains from the Himalayas; this mythical story leads Hindus to believe that Varanasi is the oldest city in the world.

Probably founded by the Indo-Aryans around 1000 BC, the city was established from earliest times as a famous seat of learning for Hindu thinkers, theologians, philosophers and poets alike. It has

Sacred Confluence

One of the most sacred places of Hinduism is **Allahabad**, 204km (127 miles) southeast of Lucknow via Kanpur. Here the Yamuna flows into the Ganges. Hindus believe the mythical and invisible River Saraswati joins the Ganges at this point. Allahabad is known as 'Tirth Raj', the king of pilgrimage places. At the sacred confluence a religious fair, the *Magh Mela*, is held each January and February, and once every 12 years India's greatest religious festival, the *Kumbh Mela*, takes place. To bathe at the confluence at the most sacred times is said to wash away the sins of many births; in 2001 an estimated 66 million people bathed here. Rowing boats will take you to the spot where the milky waters of the Ganges meet the blue waters of the Yamuna.

On the ghats at Varanasi

remained ever since a centre of the Hindu sciences. It was just outside Varanasi that Buddha's disciples gathered in the 6th century BC to hear his sermon at the Deer Park of Sarnath. Since then, Jain monks, Muslims and Sikhs have proclaimed it a holy city, building monasteries, mosques and temples here.

The Ghats

The stone-stepped embankments leading down to the Ganges River are the gathering place of more than 250,000 pilgrims a year. To see the day unfold at the ghats, you must rise before dawn to join the pilgrims. Holy men and women are up and about, busily chanting 'Ganga Mai ki jai!' – 'Praise be to Mother Ganges!'

Some are *sannyasin*, itinerant ascetics who have abandoned their homes and walked from as far as the far south of India to stand on the ghats and pray, to bathe and drink the waters of the holy river, or just to sit and meditate on this supreme moment of their religious lives. Even the most aged and infirm travel here to die, for nothing is more blessed for a devout Hindu than to have one's ashes scattered

Boats on the Ganges at dawn

in the great waters of Varanasi and thus be released from the eternal cycle of rebirth.

Practically all roads in town lead down to the **Dasaswamedh Ghat**, where Brahma the Creator is said to have made a ritual sacrifice of 10 horses. At the top of the steps, holy men known as 'Pandas' sit under their bamboo umbrellas chanting mantras and offering, for a coin or grains of rice, either sandalwood paste, flowers, or water from the Ganges.

At the water's edge, you can rent a boat and head midstream for a view of the impressive skyline, which features many Hindu temples and tapering sanctuary towers. In the 5km (3 miles) between her tributaries, the Ganges inscribes a crescent, turning north, as it is suggested, for one last gesture of farewell to her sacred home in the Himalayas before descending east towards the Bay of Bengal. You can ask your boatman to take you further upstream to the **Asi Ghat** before doubling back as far as the **Panchganga**.

Notice how the ritual ablutions, which are highly elaborate when performed by a learned Brahmin, usually involve a kind of crouching movement completed at least three times in the water. Women bathe in full sari. You'll see plenty of soap and shampoo and, on the **Dhobi Ghat**, laundry-washing, too. After all, Mother Ganges, however sacred, is also just a river – albeit a filthy one whose waters are these days officially classified as 'septic' due to all the waste matter dumped in them (see box).

Those people who might at first be reluctant to confront the omnipresence of death along the river will be impressed by the simple dignity of the funeral rites here. Families bring their dead for their cremation to the holiest of Varanasi ghats, **Manikarnika**. The body, in a white shroud, is carried on a bier of bamboo to the river's edge, where a few drops of Ganges water are poured into the lips of the dead. The body is placed on a pyre of firewood, which is then set alight.

South of Manikarnika Ghat, **Man Mandir Ghat** is home to the observatory of Jai Singh, Maharaja of Jaipur. Immediately north of Manikarnika Ghat is the eye-catching **Scindia Ghat**, where a picturesquely leaning Shiva temple lies partly submerged in the river. North of here, the sacred **Panchganga Ghat**, said to mark the

Unclean waters

It is hard to convince the faithful that the Ganges River is not pure. For centuries, those bodies not permitted for religious reasons to be cremated on the ghats – including babies and victims of cholera – have been dropped in the river while people bathe in and drink the water nearby.

Many firmly believe that the Ganges grants self-purification, a belief reinforced for some by chemical analysis revealing a 0.05 percent sulphur content to conquer bacteria. However, recent tests have shown that due to the dead bodies, sewage and raw industrial waste routinely dumped in it, the river is now officially septic, with no dissolved oxygen traceable. Samples have revealed 1.5 million faecal coliform bacteria per 100ml of water – five times permissible limits. To combat pollution caused to the Ganges, a multi-million campaign is finally under way. For the Indian government, faith needs a little help.

The faithful come to wash and pray at the ghats

mythical confluence of four subterranean tributaries of the Ganges, is dominated by the enormous **Alamgir Mosque**, controversially built by Aurangzeb on the foundations of a demolished Hindu temple.

The Town

The Chowk (bazaar) is famous for its perfumes, silks and brassware. Look out for the gilded **Golden Temple of Vishwanath**, the holiest temple of Varanasi, forbidden to non-Hindus. You can view it from the building opposite before going behind the temple to see the sacred bull, stained deep vermilion by the libations of its worshippers. The Varanasi Hindu University has an **Art Museum** with a superb collection of 16th-century Mughal miniatures, considered superior to the national collection in Delhi.

Sarnath

About 10km (6 miles) from the centre of Varanasi, Sarnath is where Buddha gave his famous Deer Park sermon (the veritable foundation of the religion) to five disciples around the year 530 BC.

Sarnath quickly became a leading pilgrimage site, attracting devout Buddhists from many Eastern regions including Japan, China and Southeast Asia as it still does today. Emperor Asoka commanded his edict-pillars to be built within the monasteries and *stupas* (hemispherical sculptures symbolising Buddha's Enlightenment), of which he had thousands constructed. But just like Varanasi, Sarnath suffered at the hands of Qutb-ud-din in 1194. Today the ruins have been well restored, and are accompanied by an excellent museum of Buddhist sculpture.

On the west side of the road coming out of Varanasi, you'll find the **Chaukhaudi Stupa**, built by a Gupta king in the 5th century AD. The octagonal tower that rises out of the top of the structure was added to mark the passage of the Emperor Humayun after his defeat in the 1540s. The remains of seven red-brick monasteries dating from the 3rd century BC to the 9th century AD can be discerned among the ruins in a pretty setting of flowers and sacred neem trees. Since its bricks were used to build houses in the town, only a platform of the Main Shrine, which once marked Buddha's dwelling place during his stay at Sarnath, remains.

West of the shrine, surrounded by an iron railing, are the stump and fragments of **Asoka's Pillar**, which was once over 15 metres (48ft) high. Notice how the shine of the granite has withstood the elements for over 2,200 years. Its inscription warns against the dissidence that could upset the important national unity under his leadership: 'No one shall cause division in the Order of Monks.'

The dominant feature of these ruins is the 45-metre (146ft) -high, cylindrical **Dhamekh Stupa**, built in the 5th century AD, which is believed by many to mark the ancient site of Buddha's most famous sermon. Below the eight empty niches, notice the beautiful frieze of fine floral and geometrical patterns interspersed with pretty birds and small seated Buddhas.

Sarnath's **museum** is a treasure-trove of superb early Indian sculpture dating from the 3rd century BC to the 5th century AD. Greeting you as you enter the museum is its famous masterpiece, the lion capital of Asoka's pillar, a high point of the distinctive art

The Golden Temple at Amritsar

of the Mauryan empire. Four vigorous lions stand back to back atop a frieze of animals comprising a horse, an elephant, a bull and a smaller lion, each of them separated by a Wheel of Law, resting on the inverted lotus that once connected it to the pillar. Against the wall is the Wheel of Law that originally rose above the lions.

Amritsar

The magnificent **Golden Temple**, holiest shrine of the Sikh faith, stands in the centre of **Amritsar ❹**, capital of Indian Punjab. Built by Guru Arjan Dev in the 16th century, the heart of the complex is the ornately gilded Harmandir, whose domes and lotus-shaped ceiling are plastered entirely in pure gold leaf. Every Sikh aims to make at least one pilgrimage to the shrine in their lifetime, but its doors are open to all and many foreign visitors regard their tour here as a highlight of their trip: come early in the morning or around sunset, when the gold colour, reflected in the waters of the **Amrit Sarovar** (Pool of Immortality Giving Nectar), is most sublime. The exotic spectacle is perfectly complemented by the live devotional music emanating from inside the Harmandir, where the Sikh holy book, the *Guru Granth Sahib*, is enshrined.

In the 1980s, the Golden Temple became infamous as the site of two bloody sieges when Sikh militants agitating for an independent homeland fought pitched battles with the Indian Army. Thousands died in what Sikhs still regard as terrible desecrations of their most sacred site. Indira Gandhi, who ordered the first attack on the temple (code-named 'Operation Blue Star'), was murdered soon after as an act of revenge by her Sikh bodyguards.

Amritsar is no stranger to mass violence. In 1919, it witnessed one of India's most appalling massacres, when British troops, under the command of General Dyer, opened fire on peaceful demonstrators at **Jallianwalla Bagh** gardens, killing between 400 and 1,500 innocent people. A memorial and martyrs' gallery at the site, not far from the Golden Temple, commemorates the atrocity, which kick-started Gandhi's movement for Home Rule.

Chandigarh

This modern city en route to Simla was planned in 1950 by Swiss-French architect Le Corbusier, who was invited by the Indian government to create a new capital for the post-Partition Punjab on a windy plain at the foot of the Himalayas. With British associate Maxwell Fry designing most of the housing, Le Corbusier created the leading public buildings and laid out a town of spacious boulevards and sweeping tree-lined avenues, inspired at least in part by Lutyens' ideas for New Delhi, and blessedly uncongested by growing traffic. He planned the town on the principle of the human body, with the

Ceremonial pomp

From Amritsar, why not travel to the India-Pakistan border at Wagah? The Lowering of the Flag ceremony is one of the best free shows in the subcontinent, taking place just before sunset each evening. Guards on both sides strut their stuff in quite extraordinary fashion.

government buildings of the **Capitol** and university at its head, the commercial town centre at its heart, and the outlying industrial districts as its limbs.

While some hail Le Corbusier's grand design as one of the greatest influences on 20th-century urban design, Chandigarh has its fair share of detractors. Many still criticise its appearance as 'un-Indian' and the predominance of concrete as not only unsightly but also ill-suited to the intense heat of the Haryana plains. In the **Assembly** building for parliament, the **Secretariat** administrative block, the vaulted **High Court** and the smaller **Governor's Residence**, you can see huge slabs of concrete-like weathered granite from the nearby mountains. The buildings boast both geometric and amorphous shapes, with bright colours visible behind the sub-breaker grills.

At the Rock Garden in Chandigarh

Chandigarh's other chief attraction, in fact the most visited tourist destination in the state of Indian Punjab, is its extraordinary **Rock Garden**. Begun in 1965 by a Public Works Department road inspector named Nek Chand, the site comprises a maze of walled enclosures, grottos and flying walkways filled with outlandish sculptures of human figures and animals fashioned entirely from junk. It was originally intended as a small garden but Nek Chand got carried away and his labour of love has since mushroomed into a giant 10-hectare (25-acre) complex, with thousands of statues made from discarded ceramic, rubber, shattered bangles, scrap metal and industrial plastic. Many of the forms were inspired by India's distinctive tribal art. For a preview, go to: www.nekchand.com.

Simla

Now the capital of Himachal Pradesh, the town of **Simla** was built back in the early years of the 19th century when the British colonial settlers were desperately searching for a summer refuge from the heat of the plains.

At an altitude of 2,130 metres (6,755ft), this was once the place where a religious ascetic offered cool spring water to the numerous weary and thirsty travellers coming out of the Himalayas. Some of these trekkers were British troops returning from the war with the Gurkhas of Nepal in 1819. They came back to build mountain retreats, as well as regular little cottages or perhaps an occasional mansion. From 1832 onwards, after Governor-General Lord William Bentinck spent a happy summer here, it became the most prestigious hill station. The British viceroys made it their summer capital, including Lord Mountbatten who pondered the last details of Independence and Partition here in 1947.

The old reasons to head for the hills still make a trip to Simla valid. Even if the old viceregal glamour has long gone, the air here is sweet, cool and clear, and the pleasure of the quaint English atmosphere remains, along with some lovely walks into the surrounding mountains – not to mention the rattling ride up to the town from Kalka on the plains aboard the antique, narrow-gauge train. However, you should expect large crowds of Indian holidaymakers during the April–May summer break.

In town, visitors can retrace the favourite promenades along the **Mall** and see the old administrative offices of the **Ridge**. The place at which these two meet is what Kipling called 'Scandal Point'. At the eastern end of the Mall you can see the **Gaiety Theatre**, one-time home of the Simla Amateur Dramatic Company, which is famous for its productions of Victorian drama and Edwardian operetta.

The Ridge leads past the neogothic, Anglican **Christ Church**, where the bells are made from the brass of cannons captured from the Sikhs. At the end of the Ridge, you'll find the baronial pile of **Viceregal Lodge**, now used by the Institute for Advanced Studies. You can imagine rickshaws pulling up onto the grounds of the ivy-covered grey stone mansion for one of the viceroy's banquets, and this is of course where Mountbattan, Gandhi, Nehru and Jinnah held their crucial negotiations in the run-up to Partition in the 1940s. Peer into the grand hall, which has an elegant fireplace, a coffered ceiling and a majestic staircase.

The most popular walk out of Simla begins just behind Christ Church, from where a lane strikes steeply up to the **Jakhu Temple**. Famous for its monkeys, it is also a good vantage point for magnificent early-morning views of the distant Himalayas.

Highjinks in the Hills

The British established hill stations wherever they could find a suitable area at a reasonably accessible altitude: for Madras, Ootacamund (Ooty) in the Nilgiri Hills; for Bombay, Mahabaleshwar and Matheran in the Western Ghats; and for Delhi and Calcutta, there was a choice in the Himalayas of Simla, Mussoorie, Darjeeling and many more. In the general relief at escaping the hell of the summer heat, they managed, in the classical British manner, to be very proper on the surface and nicely naughty underneath.

In these last bastions of the British Raj, class inevitably reared its head; each of the hill stations, like seaside resorts back home, had their own cachet. Senior officers made so-called 'poodle-faking' stations off limits to subalterns, who were not permitted to watch their superiors poodle-faking with other men's wives. For, as Rudyard Kipling put it:

Jack's own Jill go up the hill
To Muree or Chakrata.
Jack remains and dies in the plains
And Jill remarries soon after.

The Kullu Valley

The Kullu Valley on the River Beas, at an altitude of 1,200 metres (3,900ft), is renowned for apple orchards, beautiful scenery, wooden temples, and its music and dances. It offers scope for trekking, climbing, rafting and angling. **Kullu** itself has fewer attractions to detain travellers than places further up the valley. However, there are two temples in the town that are worth seeing: the Raghunathji temple, the chief deity of the

Simla, once the summer capital of British Viceroys

valley, and the cave-temple of Vaishno Devi. Kullu really comes to life during the Dussehra festival, when tourists and locals flood into the town to see the spectacular processions of golden temple deities. Accommodation should be booked well in advance.

The most remarkable temple of the valley is **Bijli Mahadeva**, 8km (5 miles) southeast of Kullu town. It is built of large blocks of stone without the use of cement, and its 20-metre (65ft) -high flagstaff is reputed to attract lightning, which, according to local legend, is an expression of divine blessing. Each time the flagstaff is struck by lightning, the Siva lingam (phallic symbol) inside the temple is shattered. It is put back together by the priest and stands until another flash repeats 'the miracle'.

The road from Kullu to Manali runs along the rushing torrents of the Beas River. It is flanked by lofty mountains and spreading forests. Near Katrain is the small town of **Naggar**, where the Castle Hotel is said to be haunted. The town has been made famous by the late Russian painter Nicholas Roerich, whose luminous renditions of the Himalayas can be seen in a gallery here.

Manali is circled by beautiful glades of deodars and flowering horse chestnuts, and it is an ideal place for walks, climbs, treks and

Trekking country around Manali

picnics. It was an important trading centre, and is now a popular resort for Indian honeymooners, as well as Western and Israeli tourists. The town is split into two parts: the new town is where the bus-stand and most of the hotels are, while along The Mall (main street) and over the Manalsu River is the more atmospheric old village, where you can find accommodation in traditional houses. The Hindu Dhungri Temple, dedicated to the goddess Hidimba, is believed to be more than 1,000 years old, while Manali's large Tibetan population has built two new *gompas* (monasteries).

Three kilometres (2 miles) up the valley from Manali are the hot springs of **Vashisht**. The temple complex here has separate outdoor baths for men and women. The Kullu Valley ends as the road passes the ski resort of Solang and winds up through rocky ranges to the **Rohtang Pass**, gateway to the enchanting Lahaul and Spiti valleys. Marking the line of the Great Himalayan Watershed, it forms a stark divide between the lush Kullu Valley and the arid mountains beyond, which lie in the vast rainshadow of the world's highest range of peaks. In 2015, work on a 9-km (6-mile) tunnel beneath the pass is scheduled to reach completion, and should radically transform Lahaul, the region immediately to its north, by providing a year-round connection with the Kullu Valley.

Dharamsala

West of Manali in the beautiful Kangra Valley is **Dharamsala**, at the foot of the Dhauladhar Range. Consisting of a lower and an upper town, its altitude varies from 1,000 to 2,000 metres (3,250 to 6,500ft). Upper Dharamsala, better known as **McLeod Ganj**, is the home of His

Holiness the Dalai Lama and the Tibetan Government in Exile. The large Tibetan population supports many organisations, including TIPA (Tibetan Institute of Performing Arts), which preserves and arranges performances of traditional Tibetan music and dance, particularly the drama, *lhamo*. In the lower town is the **Museum of Kangra Art**, housing a collection of miniature paintings and other local artefacts.

The nearby ancient town of **Kangra** is well known for its temples – whose riches were plundered by a number of invaders – the most popular being the one dedicated to the goddess Vajresvari. Also well worth visiting is Kangra's fort, once the palace of the local Katoch kings, with an outstanding view over the valley below.

Kashmir

The Vale of Kashmir, 1,700 metres (5,000ft) above sea level, has historically offered much-needed respite for conquerors and travellers alike. With its flower-filled meadows, forests, full fruit orchards and lakes, it remains the undisputed treasure of South Asia. Tourism

Shikaras (wooden boats) on Dal Lake in Kashmir

in the region, however, ground to a halt in the mid-1990s, after six Western travellers were abducted and murdered by a militant Islamist group. The tragedy was but one incident in a long-running, bloody insurgency, which over the course of the following fifteen years resulted in the deaths of thousands of Kashmiris and Indian military personnel. The situation, however, has improved greatly in recent years. In 2012 the rehabilitation of Kashmir took a major step forward when the British Foreign Office revised its travel warning for the region. Visitor numbers have been increasing rapidly ever since, although it remains a sensitive area.

Srinagar

The heart of Kashmir's capital is built along the banks of the serpentine Jhelum River on the southern shore of the lakes. Few monuments have survived its troubled history, but the city's beauty lies in its numerous tranquil lakes and gardens – best enjoyed from the comfort of a rented houseboat, over a cup of fragrant Kashmiri tea. On the western shore of Dal Lake stands the large white dome and minarets of **Hazratbal Masjid**, famous for its relic, the hair of the beard of the prophet Muhammad. There are two small squares of land that rise up out of the lake: Sonalank, Akbar's Golden Island to the north, and Ruplank, Silver Island, to the south.

The **Mughal Gardens** are on the eastern shore of Dal Lake. For Jahangir, if the Islamic idea of paradise had any meaning, it was here, amid the staggered terraces, tranquil pools, waterfalls and trees, looking out over the lake against the backdrop of the Himalayas. Jahangir's favourite was the **Shalimar Bagh**, laid out in the year 1616. A white marble pavilion on the first terrace was used for public audiences, the second was a private pavilion, the third – made from black marble – accommodated the harem, and the fourth was strictly reserved for the emperor's private use.

Three kilometres (2 miles) to the south, **Nishat Bagh** was created in 1633 by Jahangir's *wazir* (prime minister) and brother-in-law, Asaf Khan. It is the largest of the gardens, with 12 terraces and lined with fine cedars and cypresses. It has a magnificent view of the lake beyond.

Local children, high in the mountains

Ladakh

Although officially within the boundaries of Jammu-Kashmir state, the remote Himalayan region of **Ladakh** is a world apart, in every sense. Encircled by some of the world's highest mountains, the geography and culture of the 'Land of High Passes' has more in common with neighbouring Tibet than Muslim Kashmir. The majority of its inhabitants are Buddhists, and from the moment you first enter the region, the brightly coloured prayer flags and monasteries perched on hillsides of parched scree reinforce the impression that you have arrived on the margins of Indian influence.

Only opened to tourists in 1975, Ladakh is centred on the stunning Indus Valley, with a base altitude of around 3,500 metres (10,500ft). Along its floor, a string of picturesque villages cower beneath vast, ice-capped mountains. These form an all but impregnable barrier to the monsoon clouds sweeping north off the Indian plains, with the result that rainfall is minimal. Ladakhis survive primarily on a single crop of barley, watered by snow-melt channelled through terraced fields.

Tikse Monastery

For thousands of years, the Indus Valley formed an important trade artery connecting Central Asia and Tibet with Kashmir and the Indian lowlands. Along it, tea, silk, pashmina, semi-precious stones – and the Buddhist religion – was imported in caravans of yaks and ponies. The fragile – and still disputed – borders with China and Pakistan that now enclose Ladakh have effectively blocked these ancient trans-Himalayan routes, but the region still thrives as an important military base and tourist destination. With Kashmir until recently off limits, this is now the most accessible and visited of the high Himalayan areas in India. You can travel here by road from Manali – a stupendous two-day journey through some of the world's most breathtaking scenery – or fly direct to the Ladakhi capital, Leh, from Delhi. Aside from the awesome landscape, the main incentives to travel here are the beautiful Buddhist monasteries in and around the Indus Valley, and the chance to experience this last pocket of traditional mountain culture at close quarters.

Despite its remoteness, **Leh** ❺ is a developed town boasting most modern amenities: hotels and guesthouses, restaurants, cafés, travel agents, internet access and the world's highest domestic airport. Spilling from the foot of a ruined Tibetan-style palace, Leh's broad bazaar and jam of ancient mud houses looks south across the Indus Valley to the snowy peaks of the Stok Kangri massif.

Most visitors use the town as a base for excursions into the valley, travelling by taxi or local bus to the monasteries (gompas) of **Shey**, **Tikse**, **Stok** and **Likkir**. With a few more days at your disposal, you could consider a longer trip west towards Kashmir, taking in the spectacular Lamayuru gompa and the Unesco World Heritage monument of **Alchi**, whose architecture, murals and devotional statues date from the first spreading of Buddhism in the 11th and 12th centuries. The traditional halfway point on the journey to Srinagar is the Shia Muslim town of **Kargil**. In 1999, the town was the scene of a short but explosive war between the Indian Army and Pakistani-backed militants, who occupied a ridge to the north and started shelling both military and civilian positions in Kargil. The situation is now stable and the road between Srinagar and Leh open to civilian traffic. With an additional couple of days to spare, you can follow

Trekking in Ladakh

Thanks to the decades of political unrest in Kashmir, Ladakh has superseded its neighbour as the northwest Himalaya's top trekking destination. Dozens of agencies are on hand in Leh to arrange ponies, guides, cooks and porters for a range of routes of various lengths through the rugged terrain surrounding the Indus Valley. All involve long, gruelling ascents of high passes that will expose you to the risk of altitude sickness, but the rewards are wonderful views across the Himalayas and the chance to visit traditional Buddhist villages lying days, or weeks, away from the road.

Deservedly the most popular route you can tackle from Leh is the Markha Valley trek, beginning at Spitok and ending at Hemis (or vice versa). This superb circuit takes six to eight days and should be attempted only once you're well acclimatised to the altitude. A shorter, easier alternative (practicable even in winter) is Likkir to Temisgang, along an ancient caravan route.

Serious trekkers wishing to walk south towards Manali and the Kullu Valley do so via the Zanskar region, reachable in 10 to 12 days. From there, you can press on across Shingo La to the roadhead at Darcha in a further 10 days, and pick up buses back to Manali. In winter, Zanskaris imprisoned by snowbound passes are able to reach the outside world only by undertaking a perilous trek along the frozen Zanskar River – a route known as 'Chaddar'.

Pilgrims on the Laksman Jhula bridge

the largely unsurfaced road south from Kargil, past the magnificent Nun Kun massif (7,077 metres/23,218ft) and over Pensi La pass (4,400 metres/14,436ft) in the remote region of Zanskar. The isolation of this dramatic area, hemmed in by some of the most awesome peaks in the Himalayas, is set to come to an end with the completion of an all-weather, year-round road from Leh and the Indus Valley.

A day's ride by Jeep to the southeast of Leh, the ethereal altitude lakes of Pangong Tso and Tsomo Riri, where wild ass and Pashmina sheep graze on a high-altitude grassland of ethereal beauty, offer more astounding landscapes – though you'll need a special permit to reach them.

Garhwal

The mountain districts to the north of Uttar Pradesh form the new state of Uttarkhand (formerly Uttaranchal), which split off from Uttar Pradesh in 2001. Hinduism regards mountains as the dwelling places of gods, and these Himalayas, known as the **Garhwal**, are especially sacred as in them rise the streams that join to form the Ganges and Yamuna rivers. Among the highest peaks is Nanda Devi, rising to 7,817 metres (25,646ft) and India's highest mountain after Kanchenjunga.

At the base of it all, **Haridwar** is one of the seven most sacred cities of India, where the Ganges flows out of the mountains into the plains. Like Allahabad, Haridwar hosts a *Kumbha Mela*, a great religious festival, once every 12 years. The evening *aarati* (worship) of the River Ganges is held every day at Har-ki-Pauri, the main ghat.

Rishikesh, a town of temples and ashrams surrounded by forest, is 25km (15 miles) upstream. The northern part of the town, Muni-ki-Reti, is very attractive, and the best views can be seen from either of the two footbridges suspended across the river, the Ram Jhula and the Laksman Jhula.

Dehra Dun lies at the foot of the hills 50km (31 miles) northwest of Haridwar. It is a fast-expanding town notable for its prestigious institutions, including the Wildlife Institute of India, the Forest Research Institute and the Indian Military Academy, and is also the capital of the new state. On a ridge above Dehra Dun is the hill station of **Mussoorie**, home to the Lal Bahadur Shastri National Academy of Administration, which trains new entrants to the élite Indian Administrative Service, successor to the British colonial Indian Civil Service.

Pilgrimage Sites: the Char Dam

Haridwar, Rishikesh and Dehra Dun are the starting points for pilgrimages to the four most sacred places in the Himalayas, known as the 'Char Dam': Yamunotri, source of the Yamuna; Gangotri, the source of the Ganges; and the temples of Kedarnath and Badrinath.

The yoga capital

In 1968, the Beatles came to Rishikesh seeking spiritual enlightenment at the ashram of Maharishi Mahesh Yogi. Their brief but much publicised visit indelibly fixed transcendental meditation, yoga and gurus in the western consciousness, and Rishikesh has since established its reputation as the yoga capital of the world.

Yamunotri can be reached from Dehra Dun or Rishikesh. The road stops 13km (8 miles) short of the temple at Hanuman Chatti. From here there is a trek along the riverbank. Pilgrims cook rice and potatoes in the water of a hot spring near the temple and offer them to the goddess Yamunotri.

The road to the pilgrimage site of **Gangotri** runs steeply from Rishikesh via Narendra Nagar, Tehri (where a controversial dam is being built) and Uttarkashi. Gangotri, with a cluster of guesthouses that have to cope with some 250,000 pilgrims a year, is situated at 3,140 metres (10,300ft). From here it's a day's easy trek to **Gaumukh** ('cow's mouth') where the Ganges springs from the base of the **Gangotri Glacier**. Gaumukh is surrounded by some of the most impressive scenery in India, including the 6,543-metre (21,466-ft) **Mt Shivling** (the Phallus of Shiva), which rises as a sheer pyramid above the delightful meadow of **Tapovan**, across the other side of the Gangotri Glacier. This massive 40km (28-mile) -long river of ice carves its way through the mountains to the northeast, a

The source of the River Ganges

skyline dominated by the impressively pointed **Bhagirathi Peaks** (6,856 metres/22,493ft).

The road to Badrinath, home of Lord Vishnu, rises slowly from the steep valley of Deoprayag to the old Garhwal capital of Srinagar. From here the route leads to **Joshimath**, seat of the great Hindu reformer and sage of the 8th century, Adi Shankaracharya. He is credited with establishing the temples at Badrinath and Kedarnath. The Narsingh Bhagwan temple here is the main centre of worship to Vishnu when his shrine at Badrinath is closed during winter. Beyond Joshimath, at Govind Ghat, is the starting point for treks to the **Valley of Flowers National Park,** which is carpeted with flowers during the spring in April and May, and to the modern Sikh temple at **Hemkund**. The road continues up to the Vishnu shrine at **Badrinath**. The shrine at nearby **Kedarnath** is dedicated to Shiva and contains one of the 12 *lingas* (phallic symbols) of light. The temple stands at the head of the Mandakani River, in a stunning valley surrounded by snow-covered mountains.

Corbett National Park

At the foot of the Himalayas, some 300km (180 miles) east-north-east of Delhi and accessible from the capital either by train to Ramnagar (6 hours) or road to Dhikala (8 hours), is the **Corbett National Park**. Among India's nature reserves, this is the best known because of Jim Corbett, the audacious hunter of the man-eating tigers of Kumaon. The park was established in 1935 and was given Corbett's name after India became independent. The lovely expanse of forest and meadows by the Ramganga River remains a home to tigers, leopards and elephants, as well as cheetahs, sloth bears, wild pigs, jackals and hyenas. The river abounds with mahseer and trout, as well as two kinds of crocodile and the occasional blind freshwater dolphin. Bird-watchers should look out for stork, red jungle-fowl and black partridge. The forest is thick with sissoo and tall sal trees; their timber is prized for ship-building. An elephant ride, which allows you to swing through the jungle and grassland while reclining on a cushioned howdah, is a great joy.

An elephant and her calf in Corbett National Park

Rest at midday in one of the lodges at Dhikala and watch the elephants head down to the river.

Be sure to plan ahead through the India Government Tourist Office or a Delhi travel agency because admission to the park is by permit only. However, permits are very easy to obtain and reserved accommodation can be booked either in the private resorts and lodges or in the government run campgrounds. Note that the park is closed during the monsoon, between mid-June and mid-October (though sections of the park remain closed until mid-November.

RAJASTHAN

Rajasthan is one of the most romantic regions in India. Formerly known as Rajputana ('Land of Kings'), and stretching from Delhi to Pakistani Sindh and the Punjab, this is where the Rajput warriors erected their desert and lake palaces. Their fortresses were built with granite or sandstone from the surrounding hills and, in some cases, the same dazzling marble used for the Taj Mahal. Jaipur is the 'pink city', with the famous Palace of the Winds and massive Amber Fort nearby. Further east, Jaisalmer and Jodhpur both developed as trading posts for the ancient caravan routes plying the route from the Indus Valley to the Thar Desert, and Ajmer grew wealthy from the trade between Delhi and Gujarat. In spite of the droughts that have plagued the region in recent times, this is a land of cattle-herders too, and one of their most spectacular sights is the annual market-festival, or *mela,* at Pushkar held in November.

Probably descendants of the invading Scythians and Huns, the Rajputs settled in India and presented a formidable opposition to later waves of Turkish, Afghan and Mughal invaders. The Rajputs themselves claimed to have been descended from the Aryan dynasties of the sun and moon. This was accepted by the Brahmin priesthood and they were duly inducted into the Kshatriya warrior caste, to which they continue to proudly belong to this day.

While nearby Malwa and Gujarat came under Muslim rule, most of Rajputana remained Hindu. Towns with the suffix *-pur* had Hindu rulers; *-abad* is the Muslim suffix. Some Rajput princes pursued an independent line. Others sent their daughters to the Mughal harem or their sons to serve as officers in the imperial army. They enjoyed a privileged position during the British Raj.

Jaipur

Jaipur ❻, the capital of Rajasthan, was constructed according to precepts originally set down in ancient canonical texts on astrology and architecture known as the 'Shastras'. Maharaja Jai Singh II, that scholar of the stars who dotted northern India with his collections of instruments for observing the heavens, chose an exact date for moving his capital from

The Lake Palace at Jaipur

Amber – 17 November 1727 – as auspicious. He then laid it out according to the disposition of the stars and planets.

Amber Fort

But let's begin at **Amber**, 9km (6 miles) northeast of Jaipur. Located high on a hill commanding a gorge, the fortress here offered military advantage but was not suited for the kind of development Jai Singh wanted for his capital.

The road up to Amber takes you through classical Rajasthani landscape, its parched hills embracing Lake Maota, where water buffalo snooze lazily in the sun. You may also pass an occasional camel with loaded cart in tow.

The Rajputs of Jai Singh's Kachwaha clan provided visitors to the fortress with an elephant ramp. You can still travel by painted elephant up through the **Suraj Pol** (Sun Gate) to the **Jaleb Chowk**, a large courtyard surrounded by elephant stables – although the tradition came in for some serious flak from animal rights campaigners, who claimed the pachyderms were malnourished, and that the walk to and from their stables in the heat each day from Jaipur city was cruel. To improve conditions, a dedicated Elephant Village ('Haathi Gaon') was inaugurated at a village near Amber in 2010, where the animals live in more hygienic stables closer to the palace.

Street musician, Amber

A staircase zigzags its way to the **Shri Sila Devi Temple**, dedicated to Sila, a form of the bloodthirsty goddess Kali, who is shown on the silver doors riding various animals. Her statue was brought here from Bengal, where the cult of Kali is particularly strong. The **palace** is a subtle example of the maharajas' opulence: artists banished by Emperor Aurangzeb worked on

Amber Fort

the columns and arches, and on the building's gallery around the **Diwan-i-Am** (Hall of Public Audience).

The Diwan-i-Khas (Private Audience Chamber), known as the **Shish Mahal** (Palace of Mirrors), features the Rajputs' flamboyant taste for covering walls with green, orange and purple glass, and the vaulted ceilings with thousands of little convex mirrors.

The most inviting place in the palace is the **Sukh Niwas** (Hall of Pleasure), with doors inlaid in ivory and sandalwood. Inside, cool water was brought down from the roof through a carved white marble chute, and fresh air was brought in through the finely chiselled lattice stonework.

Jaipur city

The colour of its paintwork has earned Jaipur the name 'pink city', although it changes colour with both the season and time of day, from a rosy pink to warmest amber, bright orange and dull ochre.

Appropriate for a descendant of the sun dynasty, Jai Singh laid out the city on an axis from the Suraj Pol (Sun Gate) in the east to

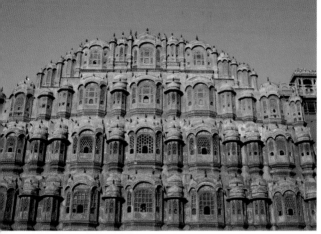

The Hawa Mahal, Jaipur

the Chand Pol (Moon Gate) in the west, a main street that is today a lively bazaar. The city's central focus was the elaborate **City Palace**, with seven interlocking courtyards. A museum inside the building gives an intriguing insight into the life and heyday of the maharajas: their rich costumes, their scimitars and rifles inlaid with bright jewels and silver, and a horrible bludgeon with a double serrated edge.

The textile museum, housed in the **Mubarak Mahal** designed by the British engineer Sir Swinton Jacob, has an excellent collection of Mughal and Rajput costume, shawls, screens and carpets. Perhaps the prize exhibit is the huge robes of Madho Singh I.

Overlooking the street on the eastern edge of the complex is the **Hawa Mahal**, literally the Palace of the Winds, but actually a rather grand, five-storey royal box, in which the women could sit and watch festive processions without being observed. Its airy, projecting oriel-shaped balconies are seen as a symbolic image of Jaipur style. There's a fine view from the top of the zigzag staircase.

Tucked away next to the City Palace is Jaipur's **Jantar Mantar**, the most elaborate of the various observatories that Jai Singh II built around India, and the final fruit of his labours that had begun in Delhi (see page 75). The initiated will appreciate the significance of its complex array of huge stone instruments, and even if you don't understand their precise function, the mysterious atmosphere of its cream-coloured gnomons (the uprights of sundials), quadrants and sextants possesses a strangely intriguing esoteric charm.

Ajmer

Ajmer was one of the most important cities of the Mughal empire during the 16th and 17th centuries, and for 2,000 years before that its hillfort – the Taragarh – was one of the most strategically important in all of India. However, the town's historic prominence is these days eclipsed by its significance as the site of Islamic India's most revered shrine: the **Khwaja Muin-ud-din Chishti Dargah**. Visitor numbers, always high, reach their peak at the time of the saint's Urs, or death anniversary, in October/November, when millions from across the subcontinent converge here to pray at the mausoleum.

Khwaja Muin-ud-din, who originally travelled to Ajmer with other Sufi mystics from Afghanistan in the 12th century, was buried here in 1236. His original brick tomb was re-clad in white marble 200 years later by the Mughals, and it was under their patron-age that the Dargah became the empire's holiest Muslim site. Inside the high-walled com-pound, through which streams of pilgrims pass daily carrying gold-edged silk and baskets of rose-petal offerings, are interred various minor Mughal royals and dignitaries. The shrines are tended by fair-skinned heredi-tary priests called Khadims, who claim descent from Ajmer's first Sufi missionaries. The hour just

A blue Indian kingfisher at Bharatpur

before sunset on Friday, is the best time to be here, when *Qawwali* musicians serenade Khwaja Muin-ud-din's tomb.

Other Islamic monuments worth hunting out in Ajmer include the **Adhai-din-ka-Jhonpra Masjid**, five minutes' walk north of the Dargah. The mosque's facade, dating from 1153, bears some exquisitely carved Qu'ranic calligraphy and is regarded as one of the finest examples of Muslim architecture in India. Across town is a fort – popularly known as **Akbar's Palace** – where Akbar and his son Jahangir used to hold court. It was here, in 1615, that Ambassador Sir Thomas Roe was received by the latter – one of the first encounters

Bharatpur and Ranthambore

Eastern Rajasthan is home to two of India's finest national parks, offering very contrasting experiences. The first, the **Keoladeo-Ghana** National Park at Bharatpur, just 42km (26 miles) west of Agra, is South Asia's leading ornithological hotspot, its wetlands and marshes alive with great flocks of storks, egrets, cormorants, cranes, pelicans and kingfishers (although numbers have somewhat reduced following the failure of the monsoon in recent years), as well as many other species, ranging from jewel-like bee-eaters to majestic eagles and owls. Vehicles aren't allowed in the park, and most people explore by bike, cycle-rickshaw or on foot, making this one of India's most peaceful and relaxing wildlife experiences.

South of Jaipur, the world-famous **Ranthambore National Park** is perhaps the easiest place on the planet to see tigers in the wild, thanks to a combination of the park's relatively accessibility and to the forty-odd tigers themselves, who have become so habituated to human visitors over the years that they will now quite happily sit and groom themselves for the hordes of camera-toting tourists. Even if you don't spot a big cat, the park is well worth a visit for its other wildlife, including cheetal, nilgai, jackals and sambur deer, and beautiful scenery, as well as the imposing old Ranthambore Fort, which sits near the entrance to the park.

Morning over Pushkar

between the Mughals and the British. The meeting would eventually bear historic fruit in the form of a trade agreement allowing East India Company ships access to Mughal ports – in effect the start of the process that would, ultimately, lead to British India.

With a few hours to spare, you might also consider the memorable walk up to the **Taragarh Fort**, which lords it over Ajmer from atop a sheer escarpment. This was originally a Hindu Rajput stronghold but now holds several Muslim tombs – essential stops on the Dargah pilgrims' trail. The views from its ramparts over the plains and city below are stupendous.

Pushkar

Hindu mythology identifies **Pushkar** ❼, just across the hills from Ajmer, as the spot where a lotus flower dropped by Brahma, the Creator, fell to earth. A gorgeous little lake promptly sprang out of the Thar Desert, regarded by Hindus as one of India's most sacred sites. During the full moon of Kartika month (usually November), tens of thousands come to bathe in the redemptive waters, and to

Jodhpur – a patchwork in blue

buy and sell livestock at the huge **Camel Mela** held in the dunes to the south of town. The fair has become a major tourist event, for which a whole town of tents is set up.

Even if your visit doesn't coincide with the famous *mela*, Pushkar deserves a detour. Set against a backdrop of sharp-ridged hills – the **Nag Pahar**, or 'Snake Mountain' – the lake and its entourage of domed temples, bathing ghats and whitewashed *havelis* (merchants' houses) is one of Rajasthan's defining sights. For the ultimate view, climb up the flight of ancient stone steps to the **Savitri Temple**, southwest of town, from whose terrace you can look down the Aravalli mountain range and across the Thar, rippling into the distance.

Jodhpur ⑧

Of all Rajasthan's citadels, Jodhpur's **Meherangarh Fort**, perched high on its sheer cliffs at the eastern edge of the Thar Desert, must surely rank among the most imposing. The Rathor Rajputs, always a belligerent bunch and bad trouble for Mughal foes and rival

Rajputs, built it in the 15th century. Akbar decided it was better to have them on his side than to try to convert them; when he married the Maharaja of Jodhpur's sister, Jodha Bhai (for whom he built a grand palace at Fatehpur Sikri; see page 82), there was no question of converting her to Islam.

Near the east gate, you'll see tombstones where soldiers died defending the fort, and cannonball scars indicating efforts by the Maharaja of Jaipur to snatch a promised bride, Princess Krishna Kumari, against her will; she took her own life during the battle. On top of the ramparts the fort displays its proudest possessions: a set of fierce-looking howitzers and a few cannons. From here there is a fine view of the famous blue-and-whitewashed city. The blue colour is popularly said to denote homes belonging to the Brahmins, or priestly, caste, but it was probably a means of protecting property from attack by termites, being made of insect-proof copper sulphate.

Behind the ramparts and the gates with sharp iron spikes to stop elephants from ramming them, there is a very handsome residential palace. Its majesty is most notable in the balconies of the **Royal Harem** (zenana), which have screens (jalis) of the most delicate pierced stone latticework. The palace **museum** displays a colourful collection of exhibits, giving insight into the daily life of those who lived there. There are luxuriously embroidered elephant howdahs, as well as babies' cradles and ladies' palanquins. A version of a sedan-chair, a palanquin was either completely closed up so that a promised bride was invisible while inside, or constructed with a peep hole to allow her to see out – and be seen – when she was married.

Great King of Kings

Rajput princes attached great importance to titles. At first they were known as Rao or Rana ('Chief' or 'Chieftain') of their clan. Akbar made them happy by calling them Raja ('King'). From there, they promoted themselves to Maharaja ('Great King') or, higher ranking, Maharana, then Maharaja Dhiraj ('Great King of Kings').

At the **Loha Pol** exit, you'll see a more poignant side of the life of a maharaja's wife – 15 scarlet *sati* handprints on the wall, from widows who threw themselves onto their husbands' funeral pyres in ritual sacrifice, in keeping with the tradition of the era.

In the bustling old centre of Jodhpur itself, you can't and shouldn't miss the **Sardar Market** situated by the old clock-tower. In the stalls around it, spices and grain are piled up in multicoloured mountains; merchants chant as they measure out separate lots of 5kg (11lb) each: 'three, three, three', 'four, four, four', and 'five, five, five'. The fort always looms on the horizon, a constant reminder of the town's war-torn history.

Just 9km (6 miles) due north of Jodhpur, the maharajas' mausoleum is in a pretty park on the site of the old capital of **Mandor**, where a number of temple-like memorials, or *chattris*, are built on the site of the maharajas' funeral pyres.

If you're going to Jaisalmer by road, it's well worth a detour to **Osian** to see the stunning Hindu and Jain temples, many of them dating as far back as the 8th century. Somehow this ancient sculpted pantheon of Hindu deities and Jain prophets has survived the sometimes ferocious weather of India and the iconoclasts of Mahmud of Ghazni and later Muslim rulers.

Jaisalmer

The city of **Jaisalmer** ❾ rises like a mirage from the sands of the Thar Desert. Until the late 19th century, it lay on one of Asia's most prosperous trade routes, connecting China, Tibet and the Gangetic plains with the ports of Gujarat and Sindh. But the coming of the railways heralded its demise, which was sealed when Partition created a closed border to the west in 1947.

Founded in 1156, Jaisalmer is the oldest of Rajasthan's fortified towns. At the heart of the town lies the original **fort**, protected by an imposing double set of bastions and criss-crossed with narrow streets and alleyways lined with ancient houses. Around this stretches the more modern town, fashioned out of the same honey-coloured stone and home to numerous spectacularly carved *havelis*

Jaisalmer fort

(merchants' houses). The best views of the citadel are to be had from the rooftops of its ornately carved *havelis*, many of which now accommodate atmospheric hotels.

The elaborate sculpture in four 15th-century **Jain temples** within the fort finds its counterpart in the finely carved facades of the merchants' *havelis*, built 200 years later, and sheltered from sandstorms on the northeast side. But much more than the individual monuments – handsome but hardly grandiose, because of the restricted spaces available – it is the general atmosphere of the town that gives it its special magic. Everything here is bathed in a serene desert light that adds a shimmer to the stone and a translucence to the shadows.

To see the **desert** at its best, go out at dawn and at sunset. Beyond Jaisalmer, you'll find the road peters out at the village of **Sam**, where streams of tourists, hawkers, guides, camel-ride wallahs and sundry hangers-on gather at sunset to enjoy the largest expanse of dunes accessible by road. Nearby, Indian military installations remind you of the proximity of the fractious Pakistan

Camels rest in the Thar Desert

border. Longer camel safaris can be set up through Jaisalmer travel agencies. Ask the camel driver to direct you to the relatively untouristed village of **Kuldhara** – one of 84 villages abandoned over 160 years ago by the clan of Paliwal Brahmins, who, after living there for centuries, left suddenly during the night, rather than having to face paying the new, arbitrary land tax. It still stands as a ghost town – groups of dilapidated square houses made from sandstone.

Out in the desert just 40km (25 miles) southwest of Jaisalmer, lies the village of **Khuri**. The main attraction here is the desert solitude and beautifully decorated houses of mud and straw. Accommodation options are also available to get an authentic flavour of desert life, and camels can be hired locally.

Bikaner

Away to the northeast, **Bikaner** was founded in 1488. Rao Bika, a son of the ruler of Jodhpur, was given an army and asked to seek his own fortune to avoid a war of succession. Thus Bikaner sprang up in the heart of the wilderness called Jangaldesh. Perhaps the very bareness of the landscape spurred the human hand to create beauty. **Junagarh Fort**, built in the 16th century, was never conquered. Its imposing sandstone walls enclose one of Rajasthan's finest palaces, with apartments and courtyards of great refinement, such as the sumptuous Anup Mahal, richly decorated in gold and red filigree.

In the north of town, the extravagant 19th-century **Lallgarh Palace** boasts acres of exquisitely carved sandstone and marble decor, while the **Old Town** is home to a sequence of fanciful early 20th-century *havelis*, decorated in an eclectic panoply of styles ranging from French Renaissance to Art Nouveau, as well as several interesting Hindu and Jain temples.

Deshnok village, 30km (16 miles) to the south, is visited by huge numbers of Hindus as the site of the famous **Karni Mata Temple**. The shrine's presiding deity is an image of a 14th-century female bard, or *charani*, who rose to become a powerful local cult leader and patron goddess of the royal family. What really distinguishes the temple from all others in India, however, is that members of Karni Mata's followers are believed to be reincarnated here as rats *(kaba)*. Thousands of the holy rodents scamper free through the marble precinct, where they're fed by adoring worshippers.

North of Bikaner, between Suratgarh and Anupgarh, are the remains of the Harappan city of **Kalibangan**, dating back to around 3000 BC. The largest Harappan site in India, Kalibangan was originally an extensive citadel on the banks of the Ghaggar River. Excavations and finds have shown, as at all Harappan sites, a high degree of social organisation, with a well-designed sewage system and a uniform system of weights and measures.

Udaipur

If Jaisalmer is the city of the desert, then **Udaipur** ❿ is its opposite: the city of lakes and gardens. The lakes were created by Maharana Udai Singh for his new capital by damming up the Berach River after Akbar had ransacked his former capital at Chittaurgarh.

Lake Pichola, 4km (2.5 miles) long and 3km (2 miles) wide, is the largest lake. Boat trips around the lake leave from the small pier behind the City Palace, allowing you to take a closer look at the spectacular Lake Palace Hotel, which appears to float magically in the middle of the lake, and the nearby Jag Mandir island. You can

Udaipur's City Palace

stop off at Jag Mandir en route, although you can't visit the Lake Palace Hotel unless you're staying or have a confirmed dinner reservation. The southern end of Pichola has the best view of the lake, taking in the two island-palaces and the City Palace beyond.

The 16th-century **City Palace** on the east shore of the lake is now part royal residence, part luxury hotel and part museum. The sun symbol of the maharana is everywhere. The armour displayed includes an outfit for disguising horses as elephants. The frescoes illustrate the tragic story of Princess Krishna's suicide at Jodhpur; glass baubles, some as big as golf balls, have replaced real jewels in the mosaics.

Most of the interest in Udaipur city centres on its old quarter, packed behind the ghats on the eastern shores of the lake. Competing for the best views, several fine havelis still stand on the waterside, including the enormous **Bagore-ki-Haveli**, a former prime minister's residence converted into an engaging museum, where live performances of Rajasthani folk music and dance are staged every evening. Up the hill towards the City Palace is the elaborately carved **Jagdish Temple**, home to a black-stone Vishnu in his incarnation as Jagannath.

A pleasant drive along the banks of Fateh Sagar – the second of Udaipur's lakes – takes you 5km (3 miles) west of the city towards Rana Sajjan Singh's late-19th century **Monsoon Palace**, or Sajjan Garh. From its eyrie atop a steep-sided mountain summit, this once beautiful royal lodge surveys a vast sweep of the Aravallis.

Around Udaipur

Although Udaipur lies within a spur of the Aravalli Hills, the watershed of the range rises 80–100km (50–60 miles) further north. Crowning one of its most dramatic peaks, **Kumbalgarh Fort**, 84km (52 miles) north of the city, served as an important stronghold for the Ranas of Mewar, who would flee here in times of war. Encircled by a vast loop of crenellated ramparts, the 15th-century fort makes a perfect destination for a long daytrip or two-day excursion, not least because of the idyllic countryside you have to cross to reach it. At the citadel's highest point sits the palace to which the young Rana Udai Singh, heir to the Mewar throne, was spirited away by his wet nurse to protect him from a murderous rival. The views from its arched windows across the plains of Rajasthan are extraordinary.

Down the mountain from Kumbalgarh, separated by a tract of dense forest where Bhil tribal people still hunt with bows and arrows, stands one of India's largest complexes of Jain shrines. Built of creamy white marble, the temples of **Ranakpur** are as elaborately carved as those at Dilwara, in Mount Abu (see page 129), though they see barely a trickle of foreign visitors.

En route to Kumbalgarh and Ranakpur, it's worth stopping at **Eklingji**, where the Rana of Mewar's protective deity resides in a grand white-marble shrine 22km (14 miles) north of Udaipur, and at the popular **Nathdwara Temple** – one of the state's principal Hindu pilgrimage sites. The latter, 48km (30 miles) north of Udaipur, was established during the 17th-century reign of Aurangzeb, when Krishna worship was punishable by summary execution. Priests from Mathura, the blue-skinned god's birthplace,

Shilpagram arts

For recitals of Rajasthani music and dance, and displays of regional handicrafts, jump in a taxi to the wonderful Shilpagram complex on the outskirts of Udaipur. Among its permanent exhibits are authentically constructed replicas of traditional dwellings, made by tribal minorities and castes from remote corners of Rajasthan and Gujarat.

smuggled their beloved deity to this remote spot in the Aravallis to escape Mughal persecution. The site is nowadays a bustling religious enclave, famous for its distinctive *pichwai* paintings depicting scenes from the Krishna story.

Chittaurgarh

Chittaurgarh (usually abbreviated to Chittor), 112km (70 miles) to the northeast of Udaipur and accessible by road or rail, has one of the region's mightiest citadels. Perched on a hilltop that rises sharply from the plains below, the citadel is celebrated for its tales of Rajput heroism. It was attacked three times by a stronger enemy. In 1303, Sultan Ala-ud-Din Khalji of Delhi laid siege to Chittaurgarh, it is said, to win for himself the Princess Padmini, whose beauty he had been allowed only a glimpse of in a mirror. Rather than submit, the Rajputs' wives and daughters committed *jauhar*, mass self-immolation, while the warriors rode out of the fort in the saffron robes traditionally worn for the last battle unto death. Over 200 years later came another heroic resistance against the Sultan of Gujarat, ending in another tragic *jauhar*, in which 13,000 women are said to have died along with 32,000 saffron-clad Rajputs. The last stand came with the devastating attack by Akbar in 1567, and one final suicidal sacrifice and battle.

Udaipur textiles

Entering the northwestern side, you can go through seven gateways to see the remains of the Rajputs' heroic exploits. South of the Main Gate, the 15th-century **Palace of Kumbha** is built over the cave where Padmini led the first *jauhar* and to which the Rajputs' descendants return for an annual celebration. Some of the walls in the palace were built with pieces of stone removed from Buddhist temples. The

Chittaurgarh fort

Jaya Stambha (Tower of Victory), 37 metres (120ft) high, was built by Maharaja Rana Kumbha to celebrate his great victory over Sultan Mahmud Khalji of Malwa in 1440. The tower's nine storeys are decorated with Hindu deities, but otherwise it seems inspired by the Kirti Stambha, an earlier Jain Tower of Fame, built in the 12th century on the opposite side of the fort. At the southern end of the site, beside a pond with a pavilion in the middle, is **Padmini's Palace**, where the princess is said to have passed her last days. It is unlikely that the mirror in the room overlooking the pond was the very one in which the sultan got his fatal peek at her, but the guides like to tell the story this way.

Chittaurgarh itself, with a population of 100,000, is spread along the banks of the River Ghambiri, surrounded by fertile plateau land where opium cultivation dominates the local economy.

Mount Abu

One of the great sights of India, the **Dilwara Jain Temples** are located in **Mount Abu**, which was developed by the British as a hill station (now used by middle-class Indians). The best way to get here is by train from Jaipur or Ahmadabad.

According to Jain tradition, Mahavira, the last of the 24 Tirthankara, spent a year here. Of the five main temples, Adinath and Neminath display the finest carving in white marble. Adinath, the most celebrated, was built in 1031 and is dedicated to the first Tirthankar. The lotus ceiling in the main shrine is carved from a single block of marble. Neminath was erected in 1230 to celebrate the 22nd Tirthankar, and the Hall of Donors is particularly fine. The 24 elite Chauhan clans of Rajasthan claim descent from a mythical figure who is said to have been miraculously born out of a sacred fire at Mount Abu.

THE WEST

This section takes in the states of Maharashtra, Madhya Pradesh, Gujarat and Goa. As well as bustling Mumbai and stunning Goan beaches, highlights include the spectacular cave temples at Ajanta and Ellora, the stupas of Sanchi and the temples of Khajuraho; there are further cultural treasures in Bhopal, and northern Madhya Pradesh has the twin jewels of Gwalior fort and the late-medieval city of Orcha. It's possible to see tigers at the wildlife sanctuary of Kanha, while Asiatic lions still roam the Gir Forest in Gujarat.

Mumbai

'Gateway of India' still describes the main function of **Mumbai ⑪**, known until 1996 as Bombay. For those who want to work their way down to the south, Mumbai is still, as it was for the servants and soldiers of the British empire, the natural starting point.

Rather than Delhi, Mumbai is the place for Raj buffs to start out, for it holds some of the most splendid and best preserved British-era buildings in India. Once just a chain of swampy, malaria-ridden islands inhabited by a few fishermen and peasants tapping toddy from the palm trees, it didn't seem a great loss to the Sultan of

Gujarat when he ceded it to the Portuguese in 1534. They passed it on to the British as part of Catherine of Braganza's dowry to King Charles II in 1661. The East India Company picked it up for a song at a rent of £10 a year for the next 62 years.

After years of intimidation by the Portuguese, the Hindu, Parsi and Jewish merchants now flocked into the burgeoning port. The island-swamps were drained and linked together by landfills to form one Bombay Island, separated from the mainland by the easily bridged Thana Creek. Modern docks were constructed, and the first cotton mills were completed in 1853, followed quickly by other

On Mumbai's waterfront

factories to install Bombay's own industrial revolution. Militarily, Bombay was British India's naval centre and, as you will see from the many warships in the harbour, remains today the headquarters of the Indian Navy.

An occasional luxury liner still glides past the great stone triumphal arch, the harbour promenade of Apollo Bunder, and the Yacht Club to dock at Ballard Pier. For the rest of us landing at Chhatrapati Shivaji Airport, the old turmoil of dockside porters and rickshaws that once submerged the newcomer has been replaced by a more modern kind of bustle. With new skyscrapers shooting up almost every month, Mumbai is the busiest industrial and commercial centre in India – cars, textiles, chemicals, nuclear energy and shipping – and a focus for the cinema and the renewal of Indian art. But this huge wealth is juxtaposed with abject poverty, epitomised by women carrying bricks on their heads to build luxury apartments, and by the existence in the city's core of Asia's largest slums.

For anyone who is not here on business, two days, at most three, should be enough to get a good idea of this exhausting city. If you need some initial help getting your bearings before exploring the sprawl that stretches in a wide crescent over 20km (12 miles) from north to south, go to the **India Tourism Office**, situated opposite Churchgate Station. Then begin just where King George V and Queen Mary did on their visit back in 1911, on the promontory at the end of Apollo Bunder. This site is marked today by the world-famous **Gateway of India Ⓐ**, a monument moving for its symbolism more than its beauty (depending on how you feel about the pomp of the British empire it was built to celebrate). Rudyard Kipling insisted in his *Ballad of East and West* that 'never the twain shall meet', but the British have done their best, perching four Gujarati domes on this otherwise very Roman concept of a triumphal arch. This edifice was inaugurated in 1924; the Somerset Light Infantry solemnly marched through it to their ships some 24 years later – the last British troops to leave India.

The Indian equestrian **statue of Shivaji** faces the gateway. It was erected in 1961 to honour the Maratha hero of Hindu nationalism who fought against the Mughals. Beside him is the **Taj Mahal Hotel**, built by a member of the Tatas, a Parsi industrialist family, allegedly when the best hotel in the city at the time, Watson's, refused him entry. Architecturally, it is also a mixture of Western and oriental styles. You can get a whiff of the old romance by taking tea in the Sea Lounge. Apart from a memorial to the 31 people who died, there is little sign of the destruction that occurred here in November 2008, when Islamist terrorists targeted the hotel as part of their attack on the city's main tourism and business area.

Rudyard Kipling

The bard of the Raj, Rudyard Kipling, son of the local art school teacher, was born in Bombay in 1865.

The Gateway of India

The Raj District

Northwest from the Taj, in the area around the Maidan that was the heart of British Mumbai, connoisseurs can appreciate the architecture that fans call 'eclectic' and foes 'mongrel'.

The old Secretariat is mostly described as 'Venetian-Gothic', the University Library 'French-Gothic', the Telegraph Office 'Romanesque', and the High Court and the Cathedral of St Thomas as 'Early English'. The architects were British but the artisans were Indian – and adept at adding detail reminiscent of Rajput forts and Mughal palaces.

The national mood is emphasised on the octagonal spire of the university's **Rajabai Clocktower**, with 24 figures representing the castes of the former Bombay Presidency, of which the city was the capital. Even the most anti-imperialist may be touched in **St Thomas' Cathedral** by some of the poignant epitaphs for those who died in the military or civil service for their country. For big Raj-buffs, the supreme example of Indo-Gothic style is the **Victoria Terminus**, abbreviated to VT and now CST ❸ (Chhatrapati

Open-air laundry in Mumbai

Shivaji Terminus). Inaugurated on Jubilee Day 1857, it served both as a gateway for India's first railway and as a symbol for all that the British had thus far achieved in the subcontinent: of its pride, power and seemingly boundless potential. It was for the station's symbolic value to modern, independent India that its platforms featured prominently in the closing scenes of Danny Boyle's 2008 blockbuster, *Slumdog Millionaire*; and perhaps why, the same year, AK47-toting Islamist terrorists opened fire at passengers on the main concourse, killing 58 and injuring 104 others. Northwest of CST is the bustling **Crawford Market** (known in post-Independence as Mahatma Jyotiba Phule). Behind the brick facade with bas-relief friezes by Kipling's father over the gate, the stalls retain their original layout: vegetables to the left; fruit and flowers to the right; and fish, mutton and poultry straight ahead.

Uptown

Beyond Crawford Market lies the heart of Mumbai, where Indians from the entire subcontinent compete with lively Maharashtrans in the **bazaars**. Among the extravagantly coloured Hindu temples, and mosques in the Muslim neighbourhoods, Jain merchants sell gold in the Zaveri Bazaar, while other streets specialise in silver, brass, copper, leather and lace.

Another famous landmark in the city is the promenade of **Marine Drive**, around Back Bay from Nariman Point to the residential area of Malabar Hill. One must-see is **Chowpatty Beach**, not for swimming or sunbathing, but because it is one of the greatest people-watching spots in western India: fakirs and fakers walk on fire, sleep on nails, climb ropes in midair, or bury their heads in the sand; food vendors hawk kulfi ice cream as well as pan, betel and bhelpuri, a spicy local speciality.

Museums

The **Chatrapati Shivaji Museum** ⓒ (formerly Prince of Wales Museum), at the southern end of Mahatma Gandhi Road, was built in 1871, incorporating elements of medieval Gujarati architecture with those of Bijapur and municipal Manchester. It houses a collection of miniatures and important 7th-century sculptures from the Elephanta caves. The adjacent **Jahangir Art Gallery** illustrates trends in contemporary Indian painting.

Elephanta

The 7th-century cave-temples of **Elephanta Island** ⓓ make a pleasant boat excursion by ferry from the Apollo Bunder. Known as Gharapuri, Sacred City of the Kings, the island was named Elephanta by Portuguese sailors. Although their musket practice damaged many sculptures of Hindu gods in the caves, enough survive to make it a worthwhile stop. Carved out of the sides of a rocky hill at the centre of the island, the caves contain some of ancient India's finest sculpture, including the iconic *Trimurti*, a triple-headed Shiva whose imposing profile has become almost as recognisable to Indians as that of the Taj Mahal.

Marathon runners making their way along Marine Drive

The Elephanta caves

Also known as 'Maheshmurti', the panel occupies the rear wall of the largest excavation in the complex, Cave 1. Although some debate surrounds the date this extraordinary relief was carved, scholars are united in regarding it as the high watermark of Hindu plastic art: no other historic statue in the subcontinent emanates such as vivid sense of power and serenity. Flanking it are more splendid bas reliefs depicting mythological scenes, while the main entrance is presided over by a terrifying, multi-limbed guardian deity *(dvarapala)*.

Pune

Pune, 170km (105 miles) from Mumbai, was once the capital of the Maratha empire. The British captured Pune at the Battle of Koregaon in 1818 and built an army cantonment alongside the old city. Among the city's attractions are the **Raja Kelkar Museum**, which focuses on traditional Indian arts; the 19th-century **Agha Khan Palace**, which once served as a prison for Mahatma Gandhi and his wife Kasturba (who died here); and the 8th-century rock-cut **Temple of Patalesvar**, carved from a single boulder of awe-inspiring size.

The northern suburb of Koregaon is also famous as the site of the **ashram** of the guru, Bhagwan Rajneesh. Known to his followers as 'Osho', the controversial holy man died in 1990 and most of his followers have moved on, but the ashram survives, albeit in a more commercial form, as an international 'Meditation Resort', complete with disco and tennis courts

Ajanta and Ellora

The cave temples hewn from the granite of the Vindhya mountains in the northwest of Deccan are among the great wonders of India. The elaborate temples and monasteries, carved with simple tools, are superb works of art in themselves; the sensuous painting and exquisite sculpture they contain make them masterpieces.

Both temples are within easy reach of the town of **Aurangabad**. Try not to visit both sites on the same day as they both deserve to have time taken over them. If you are interested in following the historical evolution of the temples, stop off at Ajanta first, where some caves date from the 2nd century BC. Reserve Ellora for a tour during the afternoon, when the caves will be illuminated by sunlight.

Ajanta

Dating back to the 2nd century BC, the early caves were the work of a regional dynasty. Having remained untouched for 1,000 years, until British soldiers discovered it during a tiger hunt in 1819, **Ajanta** ⑫ has the advantage over Ellora, whose caves were in constant use as dwelling places.

Early excavations took the form of long apsed chambers centred on monolithic stupas, called *chaityas*. However, by the 4th century AD the old Hinayana (Lesser Vehicle) school of Buddhism had given way to the more exhuberant Mahayana (Great Vehicle) school, which replaced chaityas with more lavishly decorated *viharas*. The monks both lived and worshipped in these grander halls, embellishing their walls with figurative representations of the Buddha and associated myths rather than with abstract symbols as their predecessors had done.

Of the 29 caves, all of them Buddhist, five are chaitya temples and the rest vihara monasteries. They are cut from a horseshoe-shaped cliff standing 75 metres (252ft) high above a narrow gorge, which has a small stream running through it. Originally, each vihara had its own stairway down to the stream. The caves have been numbered from 1 to 29, west to east. Experiencing just nine of them will give an impression of the whole. Start in the middle, at the oldest, then work your way east before returning to the historically later caves at the western entrance.

Cave 10 is the oldest of the chaitya temples, dated at about 150 BC. Its nave and aisles are divided by 39 octagonal pillars leading to a stupa, with an apse beyond, permitting circumambulation (clockwise movement of pilgrims around a shrine). There is no representation of the Buddha in this early era. **Cave 9**, a sanctuary from the 1st century BC, is smaller than Cave 10 and is dominated by a stupa. The two-storey facade with arched window and Buddha figures in side niches was probably added in the 6th century AD.

Two elephants in a kneeling position welcome you to **Cave 16**, one of the most important of the later caves, created between 475 and 600 AD. The Mahayana school encouraged worship of a Buddha image, which is why the stupa was replaced with a sculpture of Buddha sitting in a posture used traditionally for teaching. Look for the figures of amorous couples on the ceiling. With the richness and vigour of its mural paintings, **Cave 17** represents the zenith of Ajanta's artistry. The walls, from the 5th century AD, show the 12 stories of Buddha's Enlightenment. Buddha's steadfast resistance to temptation gave the painters of that time a splendid pretext to show the sensual side of court life as a foil to the Master's spirituality. We see him taming an enraged elephant or appearing as the warrior Simhala attacking the Island of Ogresses, while his wife Rani, holding a mirror, languorously prepares her toilet with handmaidens holding her cosmetics.

The sculpted Buddha is seen with the wheel, symbolic of his law (*dharma*), and two deer, referring to the park at Sarnath where he held his first sermon. Look for two smaller figures on the pedestal, one of which is holding a bowl for alms or offerings – they represent the merchants who financed the cave's construction.

The small chaitya of **Cave 19** is notable for the carved facade and Buddha statues in its interior and for the graceful figures relaxing in the side niches at the entrance. Visit **Cave 26** for a riot of architectural bravura – the elaborately ribbed vaulting, finely carved pillars and richly decorated shrine with seated Buddha.

In both **Caves 1** and **2** there are superb murals of bright-eyed deer, peacocks, monkeys and elephants, and also those depicting the opulent life, with Prince Siddhartha rid-

Sensuous painting at Ajanta

ing away on horseback. The masterpieces, though, are in Cave 1: two spiritual Bodhisattvas on the back wall on either side of the antechamber.

Ellora

The caves of **Ellora** ⑬ are cut out of a whole hillside of basalt rock, and conceived on a much grander scale than Ajanta's. Villagers have relied on them as shelter during monsoons or epidemics, so the murals have disappeared, but the sculpture has survived. Starting where Ajanta left off – some of the Buddhist artists may well have moved over to Ellora – all 34 caves were made between the 7th and 12th centuries. The first 12 are Buddhist, 17 are Hindu and the other five are Jain. They stretch north–south over 3km (2 miles), allowing you the option of climbing behind some of them as well as approaching from the cave entrance. As you can see from unfinished caves such as 14 or 24, the sanctuaries were 'created downwards', scooped out of the cliff from top to bottom.

The most important Buddhist excavation (1–12) is the only chaitya sanctuary here, the 8th-century **Cave 10**. The Buddha seated in the domed stupa is worshipped by Hindu artisans as Visvakarma, carpenter of the gods, so the sanctuary is known as the 'Cave of the Carpenters'.

Cave 12 consists of a vihara dormitory with three stories. Its sensual, feminine sculptures show significant Tantric Hindu influence. You must imagine these as originally painted, in brilliant colours.

Of the Hindu temples (13–29), **Cave 14** is an interesting transition from the Buddhist caves because in the pantheon of Hindu gods, Vishnu sits in a meditative pose, suggesting he was converted from a Buddha. Another two are similar to the Bodhisattvas of Ajanta. The sculpture shows a dynamic Shiva killing demons and playing dice in the Himalayas, a group of boys playing with the sacred bull, and mother goddesses with children.

The masterpiece of Ellora is the **Kailasa Temple** of **Cave 16**. With a ground plan the size of the Greek Parthenon and a structure half as tall again, this was the work of the 8th-century Deccan King Krishna I. In the process of shaping the temple and its shrines in an area 82 metres (265ft) long and some 47 metres (150ft)

The astonishing Kailasa Temple at Ellora

wide, leaving the back 'wall' of the courtyard 30 metres (97ft) high, 200,000 tons of rock were cut from the face of the hill. Whatever was saved in hauling the masonry needed to 'erect' such an edifice was more than counter-balanced by the seven generations of craftsmen who completed their carvings from one piece of rock. The sculptors created a panoply of Hindu tradition – legendary heroes and their battles, hunts and weddings.

The result is a Hindu temple on a grand scale that can be easily compared with its inspiration: the temples of **Mamallapuram** (see page 179), built some 50 years before in the far south of the country. The huge gateway leads to the *mandapa* worship hall, with the tall pyramid of the shrine beyond, the whole structure symbolising the

Stupa I at Sanchi

mythical Mount Meru, Himalayan home of the gods. After seeing the sculpted friezes at courtyard level, you can gain yet another perspective of the temple's fine detail from above, by walking along the stone ledge that leads around the top.

After Kailasa, the Jain caves (30–34), excavated between the 8th and 13th centuries, will come as an anticlimax – and this despite the prowess of their sculptors. **Cave 31** tries to emulate the style of the great Hindu temple on a much smaller scale, but the artists here were working on much harder rock and so abandoned their effort. The most interesting of all is the two-storey **Cave 32**, known as Indra Sabha, notable for the upper floor's extravagant carving and the great stone elephant, more rigid than Kailasa's (because of the tougher stone), but somehow more noble.

Sanchi

About one hour north of Bhopal, the stupas of **Sanchi** are the best-preserved ancient Buddhist monuments in India. The site, from the 3rd century BC when Emperor Asoka ordered stupas containing the Buddha's relics to be built, crowns a 91 metre (300ft) hill on the Vindhya plateau.

Stupas were originally burial mounds; Buddhists developed them into shrines of plaster-covered stone, inside which are caskets containing relics of Buddha. Crowned by a *chhatta* (umbrella) made of stone, the stupa was erected on a terrace with a fence to enclose the path. The stupas of Sanchi lay in the jungle until they were uncovered by the British in 1818, but delay in their restoration led to their plunder. Three stupas and the temples and monasteries from the 5th to the 12th century AD can still be seen.

The Great Stupa, **Stupa I**, built in the 1st century BC, envelops a smaller mound erected some 200 years earlier. It is surrounded by stone railings; in the terrace railing are four *torana* gates, off north–south and east–west axes, perhaps in order to deceive evil spirits. Formed by square posts with finely sculptured panels, the gates are topped by three architraves (crossbars), one placed above the other and decorated with dwarfs or animals.

At the time Stupa I was built, Buddha himself was not represented in human form, but symbolised by the horse on which he rode away from his palace, the wheel of law, his footprints, and the pipal tree under which he found enlightenment.

The rest of humanity is present in the form of his worshippers, dancers and *yaksi* nymphs. Despite the strict asceticism preached through Buddhism, it is clear that the craftsmen employed were given free rein regarding their joyous sensuality.

The smaller **Stupa III**, northeast of the Great Stupa, has one torana gate; it was originally built to contain the relics of the two disciples of Buddha. **Stupa II** is on the western slope of the hill. Its circular balustrade has four L-shaped entrances with a decoration of flora, fauna and Buddha symbols. Historians have noted that the horsemen are using stirrups, the earliest known example of this in India.

The priceless relics looted from the interior of the stupas are now on display at the British Museum and Victoria and Albert Museum in London, but you can see other antiquities unearthed here at the small **Archaeological Museum** at the foot of the hill.

Khajuraho

Khajuraho

This village is famous for the erotic sculptures of its medieval Hindu temples. The sandstone structures are marvels of harmony, whose true grace lies in their sensuality. A World Heritage site, the **Khajuraho** ⑭ temples lie in a wonderful rural location, overlooked by the Vindhya Hills.

We have British hunters to thank for uncovering these masterpieces, around 1840, half-buried in earth and hidden by the overgrown jungle. They didn't see the light of day until their excavation in 1923, 600 years after being abandoned during the Muslim conquests.

Khajuraho was capital of the Rajput kingdom of the Chandellas, a clan that brought vigour to love and war, as is clear in the temples they built from the 10th to the 12th centuries. The temples are divided into three groups: western, eastern and southern. The major ones, in the western group, are in a beautifully kept park with paths leading easily from one to the other. To see the sculptures at their best, go in the morning or afternoon, or both.

The lovely **Lakshmana** temple, dedicated to Vishnu, is one of the earliest, and the only one in which each of the four corner shrines is preserved. Four *sikhara* domes rise above the entrance porch leading to the *mandapa* hall for worshippers, a larger hall for dancing girls and the inner sanctuary, surrounded by an ambulatory for walking around the image of the deity. The sculptures portray not only erotic postures, but also the adventures of Krishna: in one he uses all four arms to fend off two wrestlers.

Visvanartha, built in 1002, is more compact and ultimately more harmonious than Lakshmana. Its sculptures include a flute-playing maiden and a small nymph pulling a thorn from her foot.

The most spectacular temple of the western group is **Kandariya-Mahadeva**, with three domes culminating in the great

Bhopal

The city of Bhopal, state capital of Madhya Pradesh, was tragically put on the world map in 1984 when a massive gas leak from a pesticide plant owned by the US multinational Union Carbide killed at least 2,000 and affected tens of thousands of others. However, Bhopal is far more than this. Built on seven hills and around three lakes, the city is one of central India's most notable cultural and artistic centres. Highlights include the Museum of Man, dedicated to India's indigenous minorities, the adivasi, or 'original inhabitants' (usually referred to as 'tribals'); the Birla Mandir Museum, home to an outstanding display of traditional religious sculpture from Madhya Pradesh; and Bharat Bhavan, which hosts excellent temporary and permanent exhibitions of contemporary Indian painting and sculpture, including a gallery dedicated exclusively to local adivasi artists such as the Gond painter Jangarh Singh Shyam.

The city was founded in the 10th century by Raja Bhoj. The Bhojpur Temple, even in its ruined state, speaks of the greatness of this king, as do the remains of the magnificent Tal Lake, which once covered 600 sq km (230 sq miles) and whose destruction in the 15th century by Sultan Hosang Shah of Malwa altered the climate of the region.

30-metre (98ft) -high sikhara, composed of row upon row of 84 other, smaller sikharas. Created at the height of the Chandellas' power in the mid-11th century, the sculpture inside is the most sophisticated and ingenious: *apsara* dancing girls and *sura-sundari* nymphs coquettishly yawning, scratching, applying their makeup, or playing with monkeys, parakeets or with their cheerful lovers. The Kandariya is the largest of all the Khajuraho temples and adds, with its grand scale, a special exuberance to the life-enhancing spirit of the place.

The eastern group includes three Jain temples. The most important is the 10th-century **Parsvanatha**, built in the classical Hindu sikhara-domed style and incorporating the sculptural themes of the Vishnu temples. While the religion of the Jains prohibits anything too sexually explicit, the ambience of Khajuraho is clearly contagious, and there are a lot of voluptuous, full-breasted women here.

Gwalior and Orcha

Established in the 8th century, **Gwalior** is a city dominated by its hilltop fort, one of the most redoubtable in the world. The best-preserved section is the Rajput palace of Raja Mansingh at the northern end, built 1486–1516 and retaining much of its original blue tiling. At the southern end of the fort is the wonderful 8th-century Teli-ka-Mandir ('oil man's temple'). The steep road up to the Urwahi Gate passes a series of Jain sculptures dating from the 7th to 15th centuries. The view from the battlements near the ornate pair of 11th-century Sas Bahu temples is breathtaking.

Gwalior is a good place from which to visit **Orcha**, a

Tansen's tomb

Gwalior was a centre of Indian court music. Tansen, the great musician of the court of Akbar, is buried here. His 16th-century tomb is set in the pleasant grounds of the impressive domed Mughal tomb of Muhammad Gaur, his guru. A music festival is held here each December in his memory.

A tiger in Kanha National Park

beautiful late-medieval town, parts of which look today much as they must have in the 16th and 17th centuries when it was built. It was founded by the Bundela king, Rudra Pratap, on the banks of the sparkling Betwa River. The countryside undulates gently and the builders of Orcha adorned the landscape with a palace and fortress, plus temples and cenotaphs. The architecture is a synthesis of traditional Hindu and ornate Mughal. One of the finest sights is the view of the architecturally stunning *chatris*, or cenotaphs, from across the blue river with green hills in the background.

Kanha

For the sheer abundance of wildlife, **Kanha** is probably the best national park in India and should not be missed. The journey there might be a little long, but it's well worth the effort. You can either fly into Nagpur or, if you're coming from Khajuraho, take a train to Jabalpur and continue by road. However, it's advisable to reserve your accommodation in forest resorts in advance.

The best season is February to May, when you'll be able to see plenty of beautiful cheetal (spotted deer), blackbuck, sloth bear, gaur or bison (largest of the wild cattle), wild boar, Kanha's unique barasingha ('12-pointer') swamp deer, and also monkeys galore. Enthusiastic bird-watchers might also spot black ibis and the crested serpent-eagle. But the park is most famous for its tigers, and the 'Project Tiger' campaign is battling against huge odds here to protect the king of India's jungles.

Ahmedabad

Founded by Ahmad Shah I on the site of the ancient city of Karnavati in 1411, **Ahmedabad**, the capital of the state of Gujarat, is India's fifth largest city, with a population of 5.5 million (or 6.3 million in the greater urban area). A sprawling textile and commercial hub straddling the Sabarmati River, it's notorious for its air pollution and appalling traffic congestion rather the splendid Indo-Islamic architecture in the historic Old City. Start your tour at **Manek Chowk**, where jewellery and fabric traders occupy the ground floors of beautiful old havelis with their carved wooden balconies, windows and doorways. Also worth looking out for is the local fusion of Hindu and Muslim architecture, manifest in buildings like **Sidi Sayyid's Mosque** near Relief Road. The city boasts some striking modern architecture as well.

A brush-maker in Gujarat

Hridey Kunj, Mahatma Gandhi's ashram at Sabarmati, is a set of austere yet beautiful buildings nestling amid mango trees. It was from here that Gandhi experimented in non-violent methods of political struggle. There is a simple museum displaying Gandhi's spectacles, sandals, photographs, spinning wheel and cloth spun by him. In the north of town, Ahmedabad's famous Textile Museum showcases the regional's great weaving and embroidery heritage.

Ancient Gujarat

Archaeological finds at Lothal near Dhandhuka in Ahmadabad district, Rozadi in Saurashtra, and, most spectacular of all, the ruined city of Dholavira in northeastern Kutch, carry the history of Gujarat back to the Harappan civilisation, created in and around the Indus Valley 5,000 years ago.

Tour of Gujarat

Northwest of Ahmadabad, stretching towards the Pakistan border, is the **Rann of Kutch**. The word *rann* derives from the Sanskrit word *irina*, meaning a waste, and this is indeed mostly a wasteland of vast salt flats and baked and blistered earth. In January 2001 the region was hit by an earthquake which registered 7.9 on the Richter scale. The beautiful walled town of **Bhuj** was flattened and villages in the surrounding area were devastated. It is estimated that some 20,000–25,000 people were killed, and 400,000 homes destroyed.

For those who have a special interest in the life of Mahatma Gandhi, a visit to the quiet coastal town of **Porbandar**, his birthplace on the west coast of the **Kathiawar Peninsula**, is a pilgrimage worth planning. Gandhi was born here in 1869, in his ancestral family home. With its small rooms, trellised windows and carved balconies, the house has an air of peace and tranquillity.

Standing majestically at shore of the Arabian Sea, **Somnath** is one of the 12 most sacred Shiva shrines in India. Ransacked repeatedly by northern invaders and rebuilt successively in gold, silver, wood and finally in stone, it is said to have been built by Soma,

Fishing boats and bright houses line a Goan beach

the moon god, in penance and worship of the wrathful Lord Shiva. Nearby, a temple marks the spot where Lord Krishna is said to have been accidentally killed by a hunter's arrow.

Sasan Gir Lion Sanctuary, 40km (25 miles) north of Somnath, is one of the last places in the world where Asiatic lions can be seen in their natural habitat. One of the earliest efforts at conservation began in the Gir Forest, under the auspices of Lord Curzon, who advised the ruling nawab to protect rather than hunt the local lions. Now the Gir Forest is one of the most important game preserves in India, with around 350 lions.

Goa ⓯

Time to relax – and this former Portuguese colony is the perfect place for it. The beaches are superb, offering all the white sands and palm trees you could wish for, and the local cuisine makes use of the best seafood in India.

Instead of flying down, many people prefer to take the spectacular Konkan Railway that runs along the coast from Mumbai to the

Goan capital city of Panaji (formerly Panjim). You will get a great look at the often dramatic mountains of the Western Ghats running parallel to the coast during your trip.

After Vasco da Gama landed on the Malabar Coast in 1498, the Portuguese invaded the area and seized Goa from the Sultan of Bijapur in 1510. They held the colony for the next 451 years, until finally Nehru launched an attack and drove them out.

Goa was a vital link for Portugal's colonial trade in the Indian Ocean. It also became a prime base for missionary activity, with its succession of devout followers of different Catholic religious orders – the Franciscans, Augustinians, Dominicans and the Jesuits; the latter led by the priest Francis Xavier, who came to Goa in 1542 to teach in a seminary. The traders have now gone, but the missionaries' legacy lives on: 27 percent of the local population is Catholic, and the ancient churches in Old Goa still stand.

Goa covers an area of 3,700 sq km (1,420 sq miles). As well as historical monuments like churches and the typical Goan-style Hindu temples, there's the scenic contrast provided by the coastal lowlands with their paddy fields and orchards and the rugged Western Ghats with their gorges and waterfalls. The spectacular **Dudhsagar Falls** can even be viewed from the main Vasco to Hyderabad railway line as it cuts across the hills.

The Church of Our Lady of the Mount overlooks Old Goa

Panaji (Panjim)

Situated at the mouth of the Mandovi River, the capital **Panaji** (Panjim) is a pleasant, relaxed kind of place. It is mainly used by tourists as a transport hub, but there are some sights to see, including the **Church of Our Lady of the Immaculate Conception**, whose whitewashed facade dominates the Main Square or Praca de Flores. There's also the interesting colonial district of **Fontainhas**, with leafy squares, narrow lanes, red-tiled roofs, shuttered windows, iron balustrades and villas painted in pastel shades of blue, green and ochre. Look for old shops with Portuguese names, and little cafés and bars where the locals like to hang out.

Old Goa

The 16th- and 17th-century churches to be found in **Old Goa** have been beautifully restored, but you will doubtlessly notice that without the town buildings that used to surround them, they have acquired the strangely melancholic air of old museum pieces. The town once had a population of 350,000 with some 100 churches. Nowadays the laterite stonework of the ones that remain is repainted cream and white each October to cover the mould that springs up during the monsoon downpours.

Distinguished from others by the harmonious simplicity of its rib-vaulted nave, the church of **St Francis of Assisi** was built in 1661 on the site of an older church of which nothing now remains. The fine arabesque and floral frescoes are the work of local Indian artists who excelled at the themes wholly familiar to them – this in contrast with their efforts to paint portraits of the saints, with whose images they were, despite the hard work of the missionaries, perhaps not as much at home.

The distinctly Jesuit-style facade of the **Sé** (St Catherine's Cathedral), the single biggest Christian church in India, has a certain elegance to it, despite a loss of symmetry when its north tower collapsed in 1776 after being struck by lightning. The enormous main altar, which is dedicated to St Catherine of Alexandria, shows some scenes from the saint's martyrdom in a series of sumptuously gilded panels.

Sandstone and granite were the materials used to build the baroque church of **Bom Jesus**, famous for its casket containing St Francis Xavier's relics. Located to the right of the altar, the mausoleum was designed in Florence, as a gift from the Grand Duke of Tuscany. Each year on 2 December the remains of the saint become the centre of a mass pilgrimage when Catholics from all over Goa come to pray; they are joined by a significant number of Hindus, who also venerate the shrine.

The Deep Stambh at the Shri Shantadurga Temple

Hindu temples

The biggest concentration of **Hindu temples** in Goa is around Ponda to the southeast of Old Goa. Goan temples feature a multi-storey lamptower, called a *dipastambha*; when lit up, it becomes a column of flames offered to the deity. These pillars of light came to prominence during the 18th-century Maratha Wars against the Mughals and are unique to Goa. Scholars speculate that they could represent transformed and enlightened minarets, as the Marathas battled so fiercely against the Muslims. One of the most spectacular is the **Shri Shantadurga Temple** at Quela, dedicated to the Peaceful Durga – a title the powerful tiger-riding goddess was given when she mediated in a quarrel between these two gods and pacified them. The annual festival is usually held around mid-February, depending on the moon. The Shri Naguesh, Mahalsa and Manguesh temples nearby are also well worth visiting.

Goa's beaches

Goa's entire 100km (60-mile) coastline is strung with idyllic **white-sand beaches**. The first foreign travellers to spot their potential were hippies in the 1960s and 1970s, who were attracted as much by the availability of cheap alcohol and the locals' seemingly liberal attitudes to nudity as the palm trees and surf. Since then, the more accessible of the beaches have been developed into fully fledged resorts, fed by a constant turnover of charter tourists arriving by direct flight from northern Europe and, increasingly, Russia.

Calangute, in north Goa at the centre of a magnificent 11km (7-mile) beach, forms the hub of the region's tourist scene. A cluttered market lined by bars, shops, restaurants, banks and telecom centres, it is these days popular mainly with domestic visitors who travel here by bus on day trips from the capital, Panaji. At the southern limit of the same beach, **Candolim** is a predominantly Russian package enclave, overlooked by the laterite walls and canon emplacements of the former Portuguese stronghold, Fort Aguada.

The younger charter holidaymakers gravitate to **Baga**, a resort at the opposite (northern) end of Calangute beach, where Tito's nightclub dominates a busy, brightly lit strip. Signs advertising karaoke nights and 'Happy Hours' jostle for attention with Kashmiri handicraft vendors and restaurants offering authentic Italian cuisine and cocktails. On Saturday evenings, seemingly every taxi in the state turns out for Ingo's Night Market at nearby **Arpora**, where foreigners sell designer wear and stallholders from across the country tout souvenirs.

The night bazaar evolved out of the older-established Anjuna Flea Market, still held on Wednesdays at the next village up the coast and a major tourist

St Francis' remains

Every 10 years (the next time will be in 2014) the body of St Francis Xavier is carried from the church of Bom Jesus to be exhibited at the cathedral. But not a lot is left. In 1554 a Portuguese lady bit a toe off; another toe fell off and is kept in a separate crystal box; the right hand was donated to the Catholic community in Nagasaki; and other pieces were sent to Rome.

Goa is known for its beaches

attraction showcasing handicrafts and clothes from all over India. **Anjuna** has long been a bastion of harder-edged, more hedonistic hippy tourism, with its drug-fuelled full-moon parties and techno dance music, which you can sample at the famous Nine Bar in nearby Vagator after the flea market.

North of Anjuna, development thins out after the Siolim River, only rearing its head again at Aswem, where some of the state's most sophisticated beach restaurants and clubs share an otherwise quiet stretch of sand, and, half-an-hour's drive up the coast, once again at **Arambol**, Goa's northernmost village. Beyond the reach of package tourism, this remains essentially a hangout for long-staying 'alternative' visitors. If you've come to India to learn yoga, have Ayurvedic massages or space out on the beach doing t'ai chi, Arambol will be the place for you.

South Goa is on the whole much more sedate than the north, with most visitors corralled inside one or other of the five-star resorts backing **Colva Beach**. Extending for 25km (16 miles), this stretch remains comparatively uncrowded even in peak season.

While the rather rundown resort of Colva soaks up most of the domestic tourist traffic, independent travellers congregate more in neighbouring **Benaulim**, a predominantly Catholic fishing village that has retained plenty of traditional Goan charm. It also offers the best selection of budget guesthouses in the area. For more luxury, head south of Benaulim to the Taj Exotica, the flagship among the rank of glamorous five-star hotels built behind the beach over the past decade.

In the far south of the state, a couple of hours' ride across the Sayadhri hills, **Palolem** is undeniably Goa's most picturesque beach – a gently curving spread of golden sand set against a curtain of coconut palms. Remote and unfrequented until as recently as the early 1990s, it has since become the first-choice destination for backpackers. Thankfully, however, building has been held in check by the local municipality's ban on concrete construction, and accommodation is mainly in the form of eco-friendly palm-leaf 'huts'.

A twenty-minute drive north, Agonda village lines another beautiful bay. A rank of seasonal hut camps, some of them quite luxurious, nestle under the casuarina and palm trees, but the tourist scene is less oppressive here than any other Goan resort.

Shoes for sale at Anjuna flea market

THE EAST

This section takes in the eastern states of Bihar, West Bengal and Odisha (formerly 'Orissa'). It encompasses the ancient Mauryan capital of Patna and the birthplace of Buddhism at Bodh Gaya, the great Hindu temples of Bhubaneshwar and the sacred town of Puri. After the challenge of Kolkata, you can cool off in the tea plantations of Darjeeling or in the mountains of Sikkim.

Kolkata's Howrah Bridge

Kolkata (Calcutta)

When the body of Shiva's wife, Kali, was dismembered after her death, the little toe of her right foot fell onto the bank of the Hooghly River, and that is where the village of Kalikata grew up. Along with the villages of Sutanuti and Govindpur, it was sold to the East India Company in the 1690s to set up the trading centre of Calcutta.

It was the Nawab of Bengal's attack on the British settlement in 1756 that brought Robert Clive's reprisal at Plassey and the consolidation of the British presence in India. Calcutta, with its port connection to East Asia and subsequent development of its jute, cotton, silk and tea industries, remained its capital for the next 150 years. However, the Bengalis and Kolkatans in particular were troublemakers, violently stirred by the growing nationalism. The British found it wise to move the political capital to Delhi in 1911. Since Independence, when Partition cut its jute and other industries off from their natural hinterland in eastern Bengal, the city has suffered many economic difficulties, compounded by a huge influx of refugees from Bangladesh. It remains a hotbed of radical, left-wing politics.

Kolkata's reputation for squalor has so deeply imbedded itself in the world's imagination that it comes as a surprise to find the Kolkatans are proud of their city and its vigorous intellectual culture. Bengalis are irrepressible; perhaps the challenge of coping with daily life in this city of 4.4 million (14 million in the greater metropolitan area) has sharpened their wit. Survival here is a creative art; it is no accident that Kolkata remained the country's intellectual and cultural capital long after it relinquished government to Delhi. Kolkata was the home of the writer Rabindranath Tagore, India's first Nobel Prize winner, and of the philosophers Ramakrishna and Vivekananda. Creative people still make their name here. After the establishment-minded press of Delhi, the newspapers in Kolkata seem bright, ebullient and vitriolic; while Mumbai's filmmakers are masters of melodrama, Kolkata's cinema is known for its sensitivity and poetry, producing faithful mirrors of village and city life in the hands of such directors as Satyajit Ray and Mrinal Sen. It is the proper home for the country's best museum, the aptly named Indian Museum.

The West Bank

Even if you're not arriving by train, start your visit at **Howrah Station Ⓐ**. The teeming crowds will douse you in something of a baptism by fire, and you'll soon realise that only a small fraction of them are actually there to take a train. The station is a home for many: its entrance hall and platforms are dormitory and kitchen.

Head next for the restful **Botanical Gardens**, laid out in the 18th century, boasting 35,000 species of flowers and shrubs. The first tea cuttings were brought here from China to found the plantations of Darjeeling (see page 162) and Assam. Occupying pride of place is a 200-year-old **banyan tree**, the *Ficus bengalensis*, or strangling fig tree. Some fungus destroyed its central trunk, but it still thrives, its aerial roots combining to give it a circumference of 330 metres (1,080ft).

The **Howrah Bridge**, itself a national monument recently re-named 'Rabrindra Setu' in honour of Tagore, conveys you across the river. Dating from the mid-1940s, this massive steel suspension bridge stages the most magnificent traffic jams; it is a great place at which to gauge the Bengali temperament. A second bridge, Vidyasagar Setu, spans the Hugli 3km further downriver. At 823-metres, it's the longest cable-stayed bridge in Asia and took an amazing 22 years to complete.

The Victoria Memorial

The City

Another park, the **Maidan** , is in the centre of the city. It was landscaped to allow for a clear line of fire from all around **Fort William**, which was rebuilt by Robert Clive on a more easily defended site than its predecessor. Like Britain's Hyde Park, the Maidan attracts ferocious soapbox orators predicting the end of the world, but it is also visited by the most wonderful charlatans peddling medicine and other questionable substances.

On its northern side, the 48-metre (157ft) -high **Ochterlony Monument** was built in 1828 in honour of the British general Sir David Ochterlony, whose outflanking of the Gurkas near Kathmandu decided the Anglo-Nepalese War of 1814–15. With its peculiar mix of architectural styles, it is one of many Kolkata landmarks that has not exactly taken on its new name (Shahid Minar) and still serves as the focus of the city's boisterous political rallies. **Eden Gardens**, with pond and pagoda and the Kolkata's

Movies on the move

Kolkata's clean and efficient Metro system operates Mon–Sat 7am–9.45pm, Sun 3–9.45pm. Platform TVs show films while you wait. Avoid peak hours.

main test cricket ground, are by the river.

The **Victoria Memorial ⓓ** offers a history of the bygone Raj, Anglo-Renaissance in style with a touch of Mughal influence. Its white marble was brought from the Rajasthani quarries used for building the Taj Mahal. Commissioned by Viceroy Lord Curzon and completed in 1921, it was paid for by 'voluntary contributions' from the maharajas and nawabs. More recently, historians of the Raj have reminded us that its construction corresponded precisely with the third and most lethal of a series of devastating famines in which an estimated 20–30 million peasants starved to death.

Running along the eastern edge of the Maidan, the **Chowringhee Road** (Nehru Road) marks the old European neighbourhood whose mansions once won Kolkata the wishful name of 'City of Palaces'. These days it is a busy shopping street with big hotels and cinemas, gigantic film billboards and a roadway that is choked with traffic. Catch up on the Indian avant-garde at the **Academy of Fine Arts** on the southeast corner of the Maidan.

The dishevelled **Indian Museum ⓔ**, by Chowringhee Road and Sudder Street, provides an incongruously rundown home for art treasures from the ancient Maurya and Gupta eras. The great Buddhist carvings on the railings from the Bharhut stupa (2nd century BC), comparable to those of Sanchi, are preserved in the **Bharhut Gallery**. The **Gandhara Room** displays the earliest sculptures representing Buddha in human form (1st century AD).

Dalhousie Square, on the site of the original Fort William north of the Maidan, was once the centre of Britain's imperial bureaucracy. Here, scribblers of the East India Company – *babus* to friend and foe – duplicated everything they could lay their hands on in the Writers' Buildings. It now serves just the government of West Bengal, but with an undiminished number of babus.

It takes a detective to find the original site of the **Black Hole** at the domed General Post Office on the west side of Dalhousie Square, since most Indians aren't interested in helping you. They generally see the infamous incident as having been a piece of elaborate British propaganda thought up to justify Clive's retaliation. A plaque marks the spot in an arch at the northeast corner of the post office.

Most of the major British Indian buildings prior to the 20th century were built not by an architect but by a soldier-engineer copying existing plans of buildings back home. The magnificent **Raj Bhavan** (Governor's Residence), due north of the Maidan, replicated famous Kedleston Hall in Derbyshire and was the seat of the British viceroy of India until 1911. The nearby **St John's Church**, Kolkata's first cathedral, is an Indian version of London's St Martin-in-the-Fields; look in the south aisle for John Zoffany's amusing painting of *The Last Supper*. Zoffany used the East India Company men as models, with the painter's sworn enemy, Mr Paull, as Judas. The tomb of Job

Getting around in downtown Kolkata

Charnock, the Company official who founded the city of Calcutta, is in the cemetery.

The **Marble Palace** ⑥, a bizarre tribute to Western art and architecture, can be found on tiny Muktaram Babu Street northeast of Dalhousie Square. Built by the wealthy land-owning family of Raja Majendra Mullick Bahadur, this huge Palladian villa-turned-museum has a park and menagerie of exotic birds. It recalls William Randolph Hearst's castle in California, with its imaginative juxtaposition of ancient Roman and Chinese sculpture, fine Venetian glass chandeliers, Sèvres porcelain, old Flemish masters and naughty French erotica. The odd Mullick still hangs around to play Chopin in the ballroom or billiards in the parlour.

Darjeeling ⑰

Before you overdose on the countless temples or even just on the heat of the plains, follow the wise example of the long-gone British of Calcutta and get up into the hills and greenery which lead to the lush cool of the celebrated Darjeeling tea gardens. At 2,185 metres (7,100ft), you're well placed to take in the splendour of the Himalayas – Mount Kanchenjunga situated in Sikkim, and, if you're lucky on a clear day in April and May or in late September and October, Mount Everest itself, up in Nepal.

In 1835, the raja of the then-independent kingdom of Sikkim was pressured into ceding Darjeeling to the British. The Brits believed it would be a healthy place for soldiers and East India Company employees to recover from the ills of the plains, but above all they found

The Sunderbans

South of Kolkata lies the Sunderbans, a stretch of impenetrable mangrove forest that is part of the world's largest delta formed by the Ganges, Brahmaputra and Meghna rivers. It is a vast area, covering 4,264 sq km (1,646 sq miles) in India alone, with a larger portion in Bangladesh. 2,585 sq km (998 sq miles) of the Indian Sunderbans forms the largest tiger reserve and national park in India.

The Toy Train pulls into Darjeeling station

the area strategically useful for controlling a pass into much-contested Nepal. With tea from seeds smuggled out of China and an influx of plantation labour from Nepal, the little village of 100 souls grew to a community of 10,000 by 1849. Now Darjeeling is part of West Bengal, but Nepali remains the official language and most residents are of Nepalese and Tibetan origin. Buddhists account for 18 percent of the population.

A major part of the pleasure of Darjeeling is in getting here. Although you're driving along narrow mountain roads, you'll feel much safer than in the plains because everyone takes more care.

But the best way to travel up – at least part of the way, if you're too impatient to take 6 hours for the whole 80km (50 miles) – is by the **Darjeeling Himalayan Railway**, more popularly and humorously known as the 'Toy Train', which starts out at Siliguri, not far from Bagdogra. Built in 1881, the tiny train on a 60cm (2ft) track climbs, loops and zigzags through dense forests of sal, Chinese cedar and teak which are alive with jungle birds and mountain streams. Watch for Pagla Jhora, the Mad Torrent, just after

Tea estates in Darjeeling

Gladstone's Rock (shaped like the statesman's head). Also keep your eyes open for a first view of **Kanchenjunga**, 8,586 metres (28,168ft) high and the world's third-highest peak after Mount Everest and Pakistan's K2.

The railway builders admitted it might have been safer to dig some tunnels, but they preferred to go 'round the mountain' to allow for a better view of the terraced tea gardens and the valleys plunging down to the Bengal plains. Certainly when you reach the railway's high point, 2,257 metres (7,407ft) up at **Ghoom**, the view as you hover out on the loop over Darjeeling is breathtaking.

The only relics of the British Raj are the (now) all-Indian, and still very private, Darjeeling Club, and a couple of tea rooms and Edwardian hotels such as the Windamere (with coal-burning fires and hot-water bottles at night). The real British legacy is in the **tea gardens**, which offer a beautiful setting for the town and an insight into tea growing and processing. Makaibari and Happy Valley are among those open for visitors without obligation to buy.

A drive out to **Tiger Hill** before dawn has long been a popular excursion for Darjeeling visitors wanting to see the famous sun rise over Kanchenjunga. The summit of the hill is 2,590 metres (8,515ft) above sea level, and from the observation platform there is a superb view to the northeast as the sun first lights up the twin peaks of the great mountain, and then the flanks. The peak in the distance that appears to be smaller is in fact Mount Everest; the other summit – the one that looks the highest – is that of Makalu, the world's fifth-highest mountain at 8,463 metres (27,766ft).

For a closer look at the roof of the world, consider a seven-day trek, on foot or pony, to **Sandakhpu** (3,650 metres/11,700ft). You'll get better views of Kanchenjunga and Everest and pass through forests of chestnut, magnolia and rhododendron. During April and May, the orchids will be in bloom.

Armchair mountaineers invariably enjoy the excellent museum at the **Himalayan Mountaineering Institute** in Darjeeling. It has

Darjeeling tea

The Darjeeling tea planters are snobs with something to be snobbish about. Their aromatic tea is India's best; in its purest form it is horrendously expensive, but understandably so, given that they produce just 400kg (550lb) per hectare, compared with some 1,340kg (3000lb) in the plains.

Darjeeling's dainty 'China' tea – as opposed to Assam's coarse, broadleafed variety – is taken from the top of the bush, just two leaves and a bud, and taken away to the factory where it is then withered and rolled, fermented, dried and graded. Here, planters never use the 'curl, tear and crush' method (CTC for short) – in fact, veteran Darjeeling planters prefer not to even speak of CTC – which is what the tea planters do down in the plains. The quality of Darjeeling's tea grades is reflected in the poetry of their names: Golden Flowery Orange Pekoe, Golden Broken Orange Pekoe, Orange Fannings, and Dust, which is used for tea bags.

Buddhist monks teaching young apprentices, Sikkim

on display some fascinating memorabilia of Himalayan expeditions, in particular the equipment used by Sherpa Tensing Norgay (here Indianised as Shri Tensingh), when, with Edmund Hillary, he was the first to conquer Everest in 1953.

Sikkim

Once again, a great part of the joy of the place is the journey itself, by road to the capital, **Gangtok** (1,768 metres/5,800ft), in eastern Sikkim through the most spectacular scenery: rivers roaring through gorges, deep valleys outlined by terraced rice paddies, and forested hills. To protect India's border with China and to put an end to the unrest over the Raja's autocratic rule, the region of Sikkim was incorporated into the Indian Union in 1975. The people of Sikkim are mostly made up of Nepalese and Lepchas – the country's original settlers known also as Rongpan, the people of the ravines – and Bhutias from Tibet.

The colourful Tibetan Buddhist monasteries are the most attractive sight in the valleys near Gangtok. The most easily accessible of them is **Rumtek**, built in 1968 after China drove the maroon-robed Tibetan monks of the Karmapa sect into exile. Other, older monasteries from the 18th century, based 150km (92 miles) west of Gangtok at **Pemayangtse** and **Tashiding**, are well worth visiting, but access to them may be restricted at times by the military authorities.

Bhubaneshwar

Down the coast from Kolkata, **Bhubaneshwar**, the capital of the state of Odisha since 1956, is a city of temples. Once there were thousands of Hindu and Jain sanctuaries in and around the town. Some 500, mostly ruins, can still be traced, but only 30 are visitable. Three or four are masterpieces of Hindu architecture.

The oldest temples, dating from the 7th and 8th centuries, are grouped around the sacred 'Ocean Drop' lake of **Bindu Sagar**, the focus for bathing and purification ceremonies before the annual festivals. East of the Bindu Sagar, the 10th-century **Muktesvara** is a rust-coloured stone temple dedicated to Shiva, with a small bathing tank and gracefully arched torana gate. There is great peace and dignity in the temple's proportions; the low curved pyramid on the hall of worship and ribbed sikhara dome over the sanctum repeat the classic silhouette of Odisha temples.

Lingaraja Temple

The **Rajarani**, standing on a platform at the end of a pleasant garden, is a more robust structure than that of the Muktesvara, with a more pronounced pyramid over the worship hall, and a powerful sikhara behind it.

The greatest of the city's many temples is the 11th-century **Lingaraja**, south of the Bindu Sagar. Off limits to non-Hindus, it can be viewed from an

A carved wheel at the Konark Sun Temple

observation platform specially erected for the purpose by Lord Curzon. A pair of binoculars will be particularly useful here, in order to appreciate the splendid detail of the carving on the soaring central tower dominating a whole complex of temples. It is dedicated to the Lord of the Three Worlds, Tribhuvanesvara, who gave the town of Bhubaneshwar its modern day name.

Udaigiri

Bhubaneshwar is a centre for easy day trips to the ancient Jain cave monasteries of Udaigiri, the chariot-temple of Konark and the sacred pilgrimage town of Puri.

The cave monasteries of **Udaigiri** are close to Bhubaneshwar Airport. Excavated from a sandstone hill in the 3rd and 2nd centuries BC the Udaigiri (Sunrise Hill) caves were dwellings for priests and monks when Jainism was the state religion in the kingdom of Kalinga.

Rani Gumpha (Cave 1) is the largest and most richly decorated, with carvings of elephants, maidens and court dancers.

Further up the hill, **Ganesha Gumpha** (Cave 10) is set back on an esplanade and guarded by two sturdy stone elephants holding branches of mangoes. The friezes are more sophisticated, showing archers riding elephants and a king of Kalinga reclining with his queen. Cave 14, **Hathi Gumpha** (Elephant Cave), is important for the inscription above the entrance, which details the conquests and irrigation projects completed during King Kharavela's 13-year reign, around 50 BC.

Konark

The **Sun Temple** of **Konark** 🔞 was conceived as a gigantic chariot for the great sun-god Surya cantering seawards to the Bay of Bengal. The sikhara that once towered 60 metres (200ft) into the air like some symbolic and divine charioteer has gone, but the grandiose pyramid of the **Jagmohan** (Hall of Audience), where the priests used to officiate, still soars above 12 pairs of huge stone wheels sculpted into its huge platform and drawn by numerous galloping horses. The temple was built in the 13th century, but the sikhara toppled, its porous stone ruined by storms and plunderers and by the ambitious concept of its architect. As you climb over the remains, you'll find they have a decidedly secular air. Surya was given his due with dignified green chlorite statues of *parsva-devatas* (sun-deities) set in niches facing the four points of the compass, and much of the sculpture profusely decorating the walls emphasises his life as a king – his battles, the royal hunt and life at court. The sensuality of the aristocratic lovers recalls Khajuraho (see page 144).

The wheels of the chariot themselves, symbols of the Hindu cycle of rebirth, have beautifully carved spokes and hubs decorated with kings and gods. Beneath the wheels, there are lively carved friezes of elephants playing with children. Look out as well for a giraffe, which indicates the Indian west coast's early contact with Africa. The masterpieces among the free-standing statuary, though, are the war-horses trampling the king's enemies and the splendid elephants crushing the demons.

Fishing boats on Puri's beach

European sailors, for whom the temple was an important land-mark, enabling them to keep out of the dangerous shallows of the Odisha coast (they nearly had it turned into a lighthouse), called it the Black Pagoda in order to be able to distinguish it from the 'White Pagoda' of Puri's whitewashed Jagannath Temple further south. However, after the huge sikhara tower had collapsed the British saved the pyramidal Jagmohan by pouring concrete into its core; now the Archaeological Survey of India is performing massive restoration work on the important sculpture.

Puri

Even if you cannot be in **Puri** for the tremendous Rath Yatra Festival in June/July, the town is worth a visit just to see a community devoted almost entirely to the 'industry' of its great **Temple of Jagannath**, either directly or by trading with the thousands of pilgrims who come here each year.

Non-Hindus are not permitted within the temple precincts, but you can get a good view from the roof of the Raghunandan Library near the temple wall. Some 6,000 priests, artisans and other workers are employed within the grounds. Of the four main buildings, all of them whitewashed and decorated with bright painted sculptures, the first is where the worshippers bring offerings of flowers and fruit, the second is for sacred dances, and the third for viewing the divine effigies, which are enshrined in the sanctum of the fourth and tallest edifice.

Puri also has a beautiful **beach**, southwest of town, which is ideal for cooling off – but those aren't sandcastles the Indians are making, they're miniature temples, for this is the **Swarga Dwara** (Heaven's Gateway), where the faithful wash away their sins. Be sure to watch the *nolia* (fishermen) come ashore through the surf. Although the beach at Puri is one of the best in India, the seas can be very rough, with strong and erratic currents. Caution is advised.

Patna

The capital of Bihar serves as a base for visits to the sanctuaries of Bodh Gaya, Rajgir and Nalanda, but its bazaars, first-class sculpture museum, a major Sikh temple and the views of the Ganges River

Escaping rebirth

Jagannath, the Universal Lord, is an incarnation of Vishnu the Preserver, offering Hindus of all castes the opportunity to escape the torment of perpetual rebirth. Thousands of pilgrims congregate at Puri all year round, but mostly for the June/July festival when the three great wooden chariots of Jagannath, his brother and his sister are drawn through the streets. Then, the faithful can liberate themselves by touching the crudely carved wooden deities, models of which are sold in the town.

Although orthodox followers of Vishnu insist that Jagannath is a life-giving force, in previous centuries many sought ultimate release by hurling themselves under the huge wheels of his chariot, whence the English word 'juggernaut', which means a great force demanding utter self-sacrifice.

Bodh Gaya

make it worth at least a day of your time.

Patna was already in existence 2,500 years ago, when Buddha and Mahavira were active here. It later became the capital of the Mauryan emperors, in the 3rd century BC, and one of the largest cities in the world at 3km (2 miles) across and 12km (7 miles) long. The British used Patna for manufacturing and distributing opium in the 19th century, to keep China supplied with its favourite drug. The old warehouses can still be seen by the river in the Gulzarbagh district.

The **Golghar**, on the west side of town near the river, is evidence of the more altruistic side of British activity in Patna. This great flat-topped dome, a granary some 27 metres (87ft) high, was erected in 1786 by Captain John Garstin 'for the perpetual prevention of famine', after the terrible famine of 1770. Climb to the top for a fine view of the town and river.

The open ground on the edge of the **Maidan** is where Mahatma Gandhi held mass prayer meetings. Stand in the middle of the new **Ganges Bridge** to get a sense of the effect the river has on the lives of the Indians; it is 3km (2 miles) wide here.

Har Mandir Takht in old Patna will give you a sense of the Sikh community. It was built on the birthplace of Gobind Singh (1666–1708), who called on the Sikhs to defend their faith with armed force. The well that served Gobind Singh's house is now a marble shrine. The sanctuary exemplifies piety and militancy. A priest will explain the faith and show you, among the guru's relics, his cradle, shoes and weapons. Above the sanctuary, priests and neophytes chant from the scriptures of the *Guru Granth Sahib* in a hall, now a museum to history and a record of the tortures suffered by Sikhs. The **bazaar** nearby sells cheap bamboo and leather goods.

Among its many sculptural treasures, **Patna Museum** houses an astonishing collection of Mauryan sculpture. The most famous piece is to the left of the entrance: the *Didarganj Yakshi*, a buff-coloured Mauryan sandstone statue of a woman, remarkable for her brilliant polish, her firm rounded breasts, her navel and her seductive belly and hips. It is considered one of the greatest examples of Indian art of all times.

Bodh Gaya

The site of the pipal tree or bodhi – the tree of wisdom where Gautama Siddhartha became the Enlightened One, Buddha – stands for one of the four great pilgrimages of his life. The others are those of his birth at Lumbini (Nepal); his first sermon at Sarnath; and

Waiting for nirvana

The demons did not make it very easy for Gautama Siddhartha, the supreme Buddha, to achieve enlightenment. As he sat there beneath the pipal tree for 49 days, they played the age-old game of 'good guy, bad guy' to distract him. First, they hit him with whirlwind, then tempest, flood and earthquake. He just sat there. Then the devil Mara brought in his lovely daughters, Desire, Pleasure and Passion, to seduce him with song, dance and caresses. He just sat there. They offered to make him king of the world. He just continued to sit until they gave up and went away.

Buddha's ordeal was a godsend for Indian art. In early Buddhism, when it was considered sacrilegious to portray Buddha in human form, his torments and temptations provided sculptors with a rich alternative source to draw upon.

of his death at Kushinagar. The sanctuary is just outside Gaya, south of Patna.

The towering structure of the **Mahabodhi Temple**, built in the 6th century, prefigures the gopura gateways of south India. In keeping with other early Buddhist tenets, there is no figurative representation of Buddha here. However, there is a large gilded statue from a later period inside, and behind the temple are the spreading branches and trunks of the sacred **Bodhi Tree**, which is said to have grown from a cutting of the first one that stood here 2,500 years ago. Pilgrims visiting the temple reverently drape its branches with white and saffron-coloured veils. A platform marks Buddha's seat and a set of large footprints symbolise his presence, while stone bowls mark where he walked. Hindus and Buddhists still bathe where he bathed. The museum has stupa railings, and the granite Buddhas date from the 9th century.

The importance of the Bodh Gaya pilgrimage is shown by the Japanese, Burmese, Thai, Tibetan, and Chinese temples nearby.

E.M. Forster fans can undertake their own private pilgrimage 25km (15 miles) north to the **Barabar Caves**, which were the setting for the 'Marabar incident' in Forster's famous novel *A Passage to India*. As Forster commented, however, they have no artistic merit in themselves.

Rajgir

This ancient city is due northeast of Bodh Gaya, out on the road to Nalanda, and it has been holy to both the Buddhists and Jains since the 6th century BC. As Rajagriha, the capital of the Magadha kingdom, the town was frequented at different times by both Buddha and his contemporary Vardhamana Mahavira, the founder of the Jain religion.

The surrounding green hills are topped by numerous temples of both religions, the best known being on Gridhakuta (Vulture's Peak), where Buddha is believed to have converted the once fierce warrior king Bimbisara to the peaceful doctrine of non-violence. The Japanese have built a great white stupa on Rajgir's principle hill, which you can reach by aerial ropeway – a pleasant way to survey the rugged countryside.

Nalanda

In order for you to get the most out of the fascinating ruins of the great monastery and the University of Nalanda, it is recommended that you use the services of a guide from the Archaeological Survey of India.

A Lamani woman

The first monastery in the town of Rajgir was founded in the time of the Buddha and became a centre of learning under the Gupta kings some 900 years later. By the time the Chinese sage, Hiuen Tsang, came here in the 7th century, it was a thriving university for teaching philosophy, logic, grammar, medicine and Buddhist theology. It also sent missionaries to spread Buddhism to Tibet and attracted scholars from China, Burma, Thailand and

Cambodia. It was destroyed by the Muslims at the end of the 12th century and the monks fled to Nepal and Tibet.

The museum has a good model of the original university and its monastery buildings, worth studying before you go out to the site. It also has a fine collection of bronzes from the 9th to the 12th centuries. On the excavation site, you will see remains of dormitories as well as the refectory, kitchens, baths, lecture halls, libraries and temples.

THE SOUTH

This section takes in the states of Tamil Nadu, Kerala, Karnataka and Andhra Pradesh. The great sights of India's south include Mamallapuram, the ancient port of the Pallava kings, the abandoned city of Hampi, the wonderful Hindu temples and shrines of Madurai and Kanchipuran, and Sravanabelagola, with its 1,000-year-old giant statue of the Jain saint Gommatesvara. You can also immerse yourself in the bustle of Chennai, Bengaluru and Hyderabad, and seek tranquillity in the mountains of the Western Ghats or the tropical backwaters of Kerala.

Travelling between Delhi and Kolkata, it's easy to forget that southern India exists. The attitude of northern Indians tends to be rather disparaging towards this part of the country, but a tour of the peninsula reveals a bright and cheerful people with a culture as rich and varied as their greener landscapes – the beautiful Malabar and Coromandel coasts.

The Dravidians who make up most of the southern populations don't mind being seen as different from northerners, but they don't want to be disregarded. Archaeologists can trace their origins to the builders of the first cities, Harappa and Mohenjo Daro, in the Indus Valley. Their religion included elements of Hinduism such as Shiva's phallic lingam and his sacred bull, Nandi, before the Brahmanic Indo-Aryans arrived. Driven south, the Dravidians remained not only geographically separate, but also politically independent, impervious to the waves of foreign invaders.

Since Hindus battled Muslims until the end of the 16th century, they were by no means united. The Hoysalas of Karnataka, the Cheras of Kerala, the Cholas, Pandyas and Pallavas of Tamil Nadu all fought among themselves until the kingdom of Vijayanagar (Hampi in Karnataka) emerged as dominant in the 14th century. Each of these kingdoms showed cultural vitality, exporting temple-builders together with their spices and ivory to Burma, Malaysia, Cambodia and Java. Suffering less than the north from the ravages of Muslim iconoclasts, their temples have survived in profusion and in much better condition. Today Madurai, Thanjavur (Tanjore), Belur and Halebid are principal custodians of the peninsula's ancient art treasures, while Bengaluru is in the vanguard of India's modernisation, and Chennai, though without the self-promotion of Mumbai, produces almost as many feature films.

The strong regional identity of the south has repeatedly foiled attempts to spread Hindi and make it the national language here.

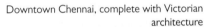

Downtown Chennai, complete with Victorian architecture

On the east coast they point out that Tamil literature is much richer than that of Hindi. On the west, the people of Kerala, who speak Malayalam, boast the highest literacy rate in the country: 94 percent for the whole state, compared with 92 percent for the next highest (the district of Mizoram); and this with a national average of just 74 percent.

Much better served by the rains, with some parts benefiting from the peninsula's two monsoon seasons, in the summer and early winter, the south's vegetation is luxuriant and colourful. There are coconut groves on the Malabar west coast, palmyra palms on the Coromandel east, and in between, a more barren landscape of rugged mountains and dramatic rocky outcroppings, relieved here and there by a patch of 'Flame of the Forest' trees, hibiscus or deep green jungle, as well as plentiful trickling streams, lotus ponds and lakes covered with scarlet lilies.

Chennai (Madras)

Chennai ⑲, known until 1996 as Madras, is India's sixth-largest city (with a population of 4.7 million or 8.7 million for the greater metropolitan area) and the gateway to the south of the country. The city is hot and congested, but the **beach**, an amazing 12km (7 miles) long, provides some relief (even though you can't safely swim from it).

Chennai was established in 1639 as the East India Company's first east-coast trading station for shipping cotton and sugar. After the defeat of the French, it took a grateful back seat in Indian affairs, far away from the turmoils of northern India. These days, fiercely independent-minded Tamil politics make the place much more lively and alert at election time.

Fort St George Ⓐ, where Robert Clive toiled as a young clerk when he first came to India, is nowadays the home of Tamil Nadu's State government and the Indian Navy. There is a **Military Museum** and a British 'relic' inside the fort: **St Mary's Church**, in the style of Wren. The most picturesque street in the Old Town, across the railway tracks north of the fort (an area once known as 'Black Town'), is

Armenian Street. Still the centre of a small Armenian community, it has a busy street market and, in a cool, tree-shaded garden, an open-air colonnaded church.

The shabby **Government Museum** Ⓑ, situated on Pantheon Road, possesses excellent Chola bronzes and a detailed collection of Dravidian sculpture and architecture. From 9th-century Pallavas and Cholas to the rich style of the Vijayanagar kingdom (1336–1565), the exhibits make a fascinating demonstration in bronze and stone of the glory of South India. Foremost among its treasures are the **Amaravati Marbles**, fragments from the Amaravati Stupa which was all but destroyed by excavators in the early 19th century. The bas-reliefs, which outshine even those of Sanchi, are widely regarded as the high watermark of ancient Buddhist art in India, though they're displayed in a gloomy hall and within reach of thousands of grubby handed visitors pouring through each week, which has resulted in considerable wear and tear on their stone surfaces.

Arjuna's Penance at Mamallapuram

The two main arteries of the city are the busy shopping centre along Anna Salai and Kamarajar Salai, where you will find the university, cricket club and **San Thomé Cathedral** Ⓒ. This simple, even austere, neo-gothic Catholic church houses what is claimed to be the tomb of St Thomas.

Mamallapuram ⑳

The ancient port of the Pallava kings, a high point in any tour of south Indian monuments, is only 60km (36 miles) south of Chennai, but stay there overnight, rather than making a day trip from the capital, if possible. It has accommodation on the sandy beach, enabling you to see the carvings, *ratha* shrines and Shore Temple by the sea in the early morning and at night.

The town is named after King Narasimha Mamalla (AD 630–68), 'the great wrestler', in whose reign its many extraordinary temples and shrines were begun. Like the cave-temples of Ellora (see page 139), most monuments are carved, rather than built, from solid rock, in this case the last rocky bluffs and boulders of the vast granite plateau that ends at the Coromandel coast.

South of the village is a set of *rathas*, monolithic shrines hewn from one table of rock. Imitating elements of the region's wood-and-brick construction, some have the same arched and domed roofs as the inner *vimana* sanctuaries that you can see at Thanjavur (see page 183) and at Srirangam (see page 184). The largest shrine, the three-storey pyramidal **Dharmaraja**, at the southern end, has 50 figures, including gods, heroes and, fascinatingly, modest subjects such as temple servants.

Doubting Thomas?

When Jesus sent his disciples around the world to spread the Good Word, the disciple Thomas was told to go to India.

'Whithersoever thou wilt, Lord, send me', said Thomas, as it is written in the Apocryphal Acts of the Apostles, 'but to India, I will not go.' Then, Gondophernes, a Pallava king on the northwest frontier, sent for a master carpenter to help with the building of a new city. Thomas' professional pride overcame his hesitant evangelistic fervour and he realised it was an offer he could not refuse. He converted Gondophernes and proselytised throughout the south, covering the Coromandel coast, where he is said to have suffered martyrdom – speared to death while praying in a cave in the southwest corner of modern Chennai.

Of the rock-carvings north of the rathas, the most celebrated is **Arjuna's Penance** (also known as Descent of the Ganges). The narrative sculpture panels cover an entire rock-face, in which a natural fissure has been assimilated as the Ganges River as it descends through the hair of Shiva.

The **Shore Temple**, which has withstood the wind and waves for 12 centuries, has two shrines, now walled off from the corrosive breezes by a line

Visiting the temple complex at Kanchipuram

of fir trees, set in a neatly trimmed garden. Shiva faces dangers at sea while Vishnu watches over the town. The temple, which would have served as a good orientation point for Pallava sailors, is clearly inspired by the styling of the monolithic Dharmaraja shrine, though more tapered. Following up reports from the 2002 tsunami, when locals reported sighting mysterious ruins visible offshore during the ebb of the great waves, archaeologists recently discovered the remnants of another temple complex 700 metres/yards from the beach on the seabed, lending credence to legends that the Shore Temple was merely one of seven such shrines constructed by the Pallavas 1,500 or more years ago.

Kanchipuram

Kanchipuram ('Golden City') has scores of temples – hundreds, if you include the shrines – dedicated to Vishnu and Shiva, and it is highly revered as one of the seven holy cities of ancient India. (The others are: Varanasi, Mathura, Hardwar, Dwarka, Ujjain and Ayodhya.) It's an easy trip of 70km (43 miles) from Mamallapuram and you can stop off to shop in Kanchipuram for silk.

The town's largest and most important temple, the **Ekam-bareshvara**, is topped by a towering sequence of *gopuras* (towered gateways) and contains an extensive array of shrines and other buildings, including a magnificent 'thousand-pillared hall', as well as a much venerated mango tree, said to mark the spot at which Shiva and the godess Kamakshi were married. **Kailasanatha** is one of the most important Shiva sanctuaries dating from the 8th century. The sandstone temple on a granite base houses some graceful sculptures of Shiva and Parvati as a celestial king and queen receiving homage from their subjects at their home on Mount Kailasa.

Puducherry (Pondicherry)

The most visible Gallic touch in this former bastion of the French colonial adventure in India is the scarlet képi worn by the white-uniformed traffic police waving you on as you drive into town. Many of the street names are still French – Rue Suffren, Rue

Painted elephant, Kanchipuram

Lauriston and Rue Dumas (Alexandre). However, only few people speak French here today. The French War Memorial on the coast road stands opposite a monument to Gandhi. After 250 years of French rule in **Puducherry**, the Indians were fortunate to have the socialist French Premier Pierre Mendès-France to deal with when it was decolonised in 1954.

Apart from the pleasant white sandy **beach**, for nostalgics of the 1960s there's a pilgrimage to be made to the inspirational **Auroville**. This utopian settlement, 10km (6 miles) north of Puducherry, was started in 1968 by a Mira Alfassa, a Parisian painter of Egyptian-Turkish descent who was the spritual partner of the Bengali mystic-philosopher, Sri Aurobindo Ghose. Auroville lost some of its dynamism because of squabbles following the death of Alfassa, known to Aurobindo's acolytes as simply 'The Mother'. But the 'organic' forms of the buildings, with names like Hope, Fraternity and Aspiration, still have an impact on the landscape.

Thanjavur

Known to the British as Tanjore, this was the historic capital of the great Chola kingdom that spread Tamil culture to Myanmar, China and Southeast Asia. The extent of the influence of its artful sculpture and architecture can be seen to this day in the temples of Cambodia, Thailand and Java. Commercial enterprise, military power and religious fervour went together. More than the divinity of Shiva, the architecture of the 11th-century **Temple of Brihadisvara** celebrates the victory of the great Chola kingdom over the Pallavas of Kanchipuram and the Cheras of Kerala. The accent is on the grandiose: the temple's main vimana shrine consisting of a massive, 13-tiered pyramid some 61 metres (200ft) high.

Shiva's sacred bull, Nandi, is built on a similarly colossal scale, as is the phallic lingam, believed to be the biggest in India. Frescoes insist (in gory detail) that head-chopping was necessary to achieve victory. However, a much more graceful architectural touch can be seen in the panels of Shiva demonstrating the 108 basic poses performed in the sacred dance, *bharatanatyam*.

Tiruchirapalli (Trichy)

The official, Indianised name of this town is **Tiruchirapalli**, 'City of the Sacred Rock', but the place is still identified by its colonial name, Trichy, a short form of the equally European name Trichinopoly. Today it is a base for pilgrims visiting Tamil Nadu's great temple complexes at nearby Srirangam, but every schoolchild, at least those from the old school, knew Trichy for the British defeats of the French here in the 1750s.

The famed **Rock Fort** looms over the city from atop the great solid granite hill that gave the town its name. From early days, the impregnable rock served as a sanctuary, graced by temples and cave-shrines. Steep steps bring you up to the Hall of a Thousand Pillars, as well as the shrine of Shiva and the Temple of Ganesh, from which there is a fine view over the Kaveri (Cauvery) River, the towers of Srirangam and the plains beyond. On the way up, look for the 7th-century, stout-pillared Pallava cave-shrines.

The French legacy is discernable in Trichy, with the Jesuit College of St Joseph and the adjoining red-and-buff neogothic church of Our Lady of Lourdes.

Srirangam

The numerous temple precincts of **Sri Ranganathaswami**, set on an island formed by two arms of the Kaveri River at Srirangam, 5km (3 miles) from Trichy, enclose a complete township of busy shops, booths and dwellings. Beyond the town's outside wall are the temple's farmland and the coconut plantations, and a large, square, lotus-covered bathing tank.

The temple itself, dedicated to Vishnu and already a theological centre by the 11th century, was founded a couple of thousand years ago – tradition takes it back to the Flood. Its present form comprises a total of seven concentric enclosures, culminating in an inner sanctum, and dates from the 15th and 16th centuries, after it had been liberated from Muslim invaders who had previously used it as a fortress. However, many of the sanctuaries are in fact much older than this.

Enter on the south side and proceed through an ornamented *gopura* gate-tower characteristic of south Indian architecture. Next, pass under a series of soaring gopuras, where you can witness religion as a full-time daily occupation. The streets are crammed with vendors selling shrine offerings of sweets, curds and coconut, as well as garlands and holy images. Elsewhere, men are cleaning the stables for the temple elephants and the storehouses for the chariot-shrines that carry the deities through the streets during the festivals. Look out for the handsome pillared verandas of the dwellings.

Temple of Brihadisvara

On the south side of the fourth courtyard is the **Temple of Venugopala Krishnan**, with its charmingly sculpted figures in the famous Hoysala style of the temples at Belur and Halebid – notice the young woman with the parakeet, which served in Indian literature as a bearer of messages between passionate lovers. Non-Hindus can proceed as far as the sixth wall, but not into the golden-topped vimana, the inner sanctum, and its arched roof with the god Vishnu portrayed on each side.

Most spectacular of all, though, set in the eastern courtyard of the fourth enclosure, is the famous **Sesharayar Mandapa** (worship hall) with eight carved pillars of rearing horses bearing proud warriors. The energy of these minutely detailed sculptures from the 16th century, which honour the military prowess of the then-great Vijayanagar kingdom, is a zenith of south Indian art.

Intricate carvings
at Madurai

Madurai

The ancient capital of the Pandya kings and one of the world's oldest cities, **Madurai** ㉑ is still an important repository of Tamil culture. Today it is a bustling university town, Tamil Nadu's second largest after Chennai.

The feverish religious activity around the nine towering gopuras of the **Meenakshi Temple**, 17th century in its present form, may give you a sense of the intensity of Hinduism. Its **Meenakshi Shrine** is dedicated to a pre-Hindu 'fish-eyed goddess' taken into the pantheon with her husband, Shiva, whose **Sundaresvara** Shrine is next door. The Madurai festivals in April and May celebrate their marriage as a grand reconciliation with the Indo-Aryan invaders.

You can get a good overall view of the site by climbing the steps to the top of the **south gopura**. At ground level notice the arcaded **Golden Lotus Tank** and the bathing place. At the west end is a detailed model of the whole site.

The busiest place in the entire complex is the **Kambattadi Mandapa**, the ambulatory to the Sundaresvara shrine. Worshippers in procession prostrate themselves, bringing offerings of coconut and fruit, and toss tiny balls of butter onto blackened statues of Shiva.

The **Hall of 1,000 Pillars** (in fact only 997) is in the northeast corner of the complex. It is full of carved, bizarre lion-elephants, and the Pandava brothers, the heroes from the *Mahabharata* epic from whom the Madurai Pandyas claim descent.

Outside the eastern wall is the **Pudhu Mandapa**, the Hall of Audience of Tirumalai Nayak, the temple's builder. It is now a bustling bazaar with various artisans plying their trade.

Stop off at **Tirumalai's Palace**, about 1km (0.5 mile) southeast of the Great Temple. An elegant relic of former splendour, the 17th-century palace boasts cusped arches and massive pillars modelled on the style of the great Rajput palaces of Rajasthan, but also some unmistakably tubby Dravidian gods on a frieze running around the courtyard.

Thiruvananthapuram (Trivandrum) and Kovalam

India's southernmost point is **Kanniyakumari**, where the Arabian Sea and Indian Ocean meet. There is nothing between you and Antarctica here. If your timing is right, you might get to see the full moon rising at the same time as the sun is setting.

A little further round the coast is the Kerala state border and then **Thiruvananthapuram**, the sizeable state capital. Its international airport is a popular transit destination for Indians and foreigners

Cruising Kerala's backwaters

In Kerala state, many tourists take the boats between **Kollam** (Quilon) and **Alappuzha** (Alleppey) along the picturesque backwaters. Cruises are run by the District Tourism Promotion Council and Alleppey Tourism among other operators (the trip lasts up to eight hours depending on route).

Made of jakwood planks sewn together with coir rope, *kettuvallam* (literally tied boats) formerly transported rice and other produce from the backwaters to the region's sea ports. Now, hundreds chug around the backwaters with tourists reclined under their coir and palm-thatch canopies. Progress is often slower than by road as the waterways can be unexpectedly shallow and are often choked with waterlilies and duckweed. Cruises typically last 24 hours, with an overnight stay at a remote riverbank deep in the backwaters.

alike. Built on seven hills, the city is named after the fabled serpent god, Anantha, on whom Lord Vishnu reclines. Created by the former rulers, the Maharajas of Travancore, Vishnu's temple, Sri Padmanabhaswamy, still dominates the old part of the city. The shrine, whose Tamil-style gateway towers shimmers to magical effect in the adjacent bathing tank, made international headlines in 2011 when its treasury was found to contain a vast hoard of antique gold and precious stones, valued at a staggering $40–200 billion. A decision has yet to be made on what to do with the treasure – many in Kerala would like to see it displayed in a special museum – but its most likely resting place will be the secret vault under the deity where it was discovered.

A selection of rather less valuable heirlooms belonging to the Travancore royal family, the traditional custodians of the temple, can be seen at their city residence nearby, the **Puttan Malika Palace**.

Just 15km (9 miles) south of Thiruvananthapuram is the popular beach resort of **Kovalam**, complete with coconut palms, papaya, bananas, white sand and surf (beware of the strong currents).

Varkala, 54km (32 miles) north of Trivandrum, is an attractive village and has a fine sandy beach at the base of striking red cliffs. Watch out for fishing lines or nets that are dragged from the sea at around sunset. About 20km (12 miles) north of Varkala is **Kollam**, a cashew nut port which is the southern gateway to Kerala's famous **backwaters**. Travellers can journey through a network of narrow canals and wide lakes where people paddle to their daily tasks. Unlike the wave-tossed western seashore, which runs roughly parallel, the backwaters are calm. Boats of all descriptions are punted or sailed along the shallow green waterways.

Kochi (Cochin)

One of the most charming towns in India, where Christians, Jews, Muslims and Hindus live in much greater harmony than they seem to manage elsewhere, **Kochi** ㉒ makes a delightful gateway to the Malabar coast and the relaxed life of Kerala.

Paddling along one of Kerala's backwaters

On a peninsula separated from the mainland by islands, the old part of the town is known as **Fort Cochin**, where Pedro Alvares Cabral set up the first Portuguese trading post in 1500. Vasco da Gama also came here in the early 1500s, during the Portuguese campaign against the Zamorin of Calicut, further north. He was buried in the **Church of St Francis**, the only Portuguese building still standing here which was subsequently converted by the Dutch to a Protestant church. The great navigator's remains were returned to Portugal in 1538 but his tombstone can still be seen on the south side of the church, set in the floor with a brass rail.

At the water's edge on the tip of the peninsula, you can see the fishermen's beautiful cantilevered **Chinese fishing nets**, a system imported from the China seas: fishermen sling the nets over a pyramid of four poles which is then lowered into the water and hoisted out again by a system of rock weights and cantilevers.

The **Jewish quarter**, referred to as 'Jew Town', is in Mattanchery, southeast of the fort. In the narrow streets lined with merchants' and tailors' shops, the Star of David, menorahs and Jewish names

Chinese dipping nets,
near Kochi

are now more plentiful than Jewish people themselves. At Independence there were a few thousand, but when the State of Israel was founded, a massive emigration left only an ageing population of around a dozen behind. The synagogue, with its red tabernacle and Chinese tiling, was built in 1568. You can see the copper plates giving land rights to a Jewish community on the coast back in AD 379.

At **Bolghatty Island** in the Kochi lagoon, visitors may take tea in the elegant Dutch governor's mansion, now a government hotel.

Western Ghats

Inland, roads run due east and rise into the forest-covered **Western Ghats**. The road from Kochi leads up to **Munnar**, an old colonial hill station and the highest town in Kerala at 1,800 metres (6,000ft), surrounded by rolling hills with neatly clipped **tea gardens**. You can go wandering through the tea gardens at leisure, and there's plenty of accommodation locally. Nearby is the **Eravikulam National Park**, home of the endangered Nilgiri Tahr, the only species of ibex to be found south of the Himalayas, as well as elephants, gaurs, sambhar and lion-tailed macaques. This is also trekking country, dominated by the craggy **Anamundi**, the highest peak in southern India at 2,695 metres (8,842ft).

Wildlife enthusiasts should also make a point of visiting the nature reserve at **Periyar**, a drive of 194km (120 miles) from Kochi, via the busy Christian town of Kottayam. Here, elephants, bison and birds can be seen from the unique vantage point of an artificial lake. Look for the elephants with their trunks raised like snorkels.

Bengaluru (Bangalore)

Modern and efficient, the capital of Karnataka is a convenient gateway to the western half of the peninsula.

Under the former British Raj, Bengaluru (which changed its official name from Bangalore in November 2006), at an altitude of 930 metres (3,000ft), was the summer refuge for its Madras-based officials, who with their parks and greenery had made it the 'garden city'. The spectacular growth of India's boom town in electronics, software, telecommunications, back-office and call-centre support has not only greatly increased the population (to over 9.6 million) but has noticeably changed the climate; it is several degrees hotter here now than it was 30 years ago. However, there are still pleasant walks to be had in **Cubbon Park** and in the terraced greenery of the botanical gardens of **Lalbagh**.

Flanked by striking boulder hills of golden coloured basalt, the Bengaluru–Mysore road provides a delightful introduction to the

Malabar's Jews

The first Jews arrived here from Palestine on the Malabar coast, at nearby Kodungallur (Cranganore), in the early centuries of the Christian era. Far from Roman persecutors, they traded peacefully with the Hindus or with Arab merchants from the Persian Gulf. In time, their community was reinforced by new refugees from Babylon and Persia and then by others expelled from Spain and Portugal in 1492, spreading out along the coast.

However, the Portuguese settled there, too, bringing their Inquisition with them and upsetting the hitherto friendly Muslims. The Jews then promptly moved to Kochi, under the protection of the local Hindu raja. The Portuguese came down from Goa to smash the synagogue in 1662, but it was restored two years later. Today, with all but a few aged Jews resettled in Israel, there's no kosher butcher left in the town and little other trace of the Jewish population apart from their monuments.

The Maharaja's Palace at Mysore

Deccan Plateau. Leading you along tributary streams of the Kaveri (Cauvery) River, past groves of mango trees, sugar cane fields and rice paddies, it is suddenly broken by the soaring mountain of solid granite which director David Lean made the location for the fateful picnic in his film of E.M. Forster's novel *A Passage to India*. You can visit Srirangapatnam and Somnathpur on the way.

Mysore

The home town of the maharajas regains a flicker of its former glory every October during the Dussehra festival, when the present Maharaja of Mysore State is paraded through the streets on his golden throne, surrounded by gorgeously caparisoned elephants.

Mysore remains a pleasant city, famous for its sandalwood and frangipani, jasmine and musk. The **Maharaja's Palace** is a museum by day and lit up at night, with the most striking decoration reserved for the annual Diwwali celebration. It was constructed in 1897 (after its predecessor was burned down) and represents all the excesses of Mughal nostalgia and undigested Victoriana. Doors of solid silver open onto the multicoloured, stylish decor of marble, mahogany and ivory. The highlight is an art gallery, with paintings of the maharajas in very British, landed-gentry poses, and a glass case featuring a 'rolled gold replica of the British crown' set next to a teapot.

On the summit of the **Chamundi Hill**, the Sri Chamundeswari Temple offers a fine view of Mysore. On your way back down the hill, take a look at the massive black **Nandi** bull, Shiva's sacred vehicle (*vahana*), with chains and bells that are a mixture of both real and sculpted items hung around its neck.

Another popular sight are the **Brindavan Gardens**, in Mughal style, some 19km (12 miles) north of Mysore, worth visiting at night when the fountains are flood-lit.

Srirangapatnam

The names of many southern towns seem longer than their main streets. Situated due east of Mysore, **Srirangapatnam** was the site of the battles against the Muslim ruler Tipu Sultan in the 1790s, in which the British gained control of the peninsula.

The fort, which was taken by Lord Cornwallis and Colonel Arthur Wellesley (the Iron Duke with the rubber boots), no longer stands today, but the sultan's summer palace, **Darya Daulat Bagh**, has been preserved and made into a museum honouring the brave resistance of Tipu and his father, Haidar Ali.

Somnathpur

The **Kesava Temple** at **Somnathpur**, built in 1268, is considered one of the greatest examples of the Hoysala style. The structure is small, no more than 10 metres (30ft) high, and its vimanas (shrines) are set on a low, modest platform, but the temple achieves a grandeur in miniature, peacefully enclosed in its courtyard and isolated from the rest of the village. It is a tiny, shining jewel in the crown of Indian architecture.

The temple has been dedicated to Vishnu in his various aspects: as Janardana the Punisher, shown as a rigid, solemn-looking statue

Belur temple carving.

on the north vimana; as Kesava the Radiant, after whom the temple is named but whose statue is missing from the central shrine; and as Venugopala, the Krishna on the south shrine, with another Krishna (the cowherd) listening at his feet.

With a domed sikhara on each shrine, the temple's overall effect remains 'horizontal' in the style of the Hoysala kingdom, emphasised by the layers of narrow, parallel carved friezes running around the walls. Every square centimetre of the temple's surface is sculpted. An unusual feature in the Hoysala temples is that their carvings are signed by the sculptors. Like the statues of romanesque and gothic cathedrals portraying events from the Bible, the carvings were intended to be read like a book by those who had no access to the scriptures, which were at that time reserved for the Brahmins. They tell the stories of the gods – of the mischievous tricks of Krishna, as a child stealing butter from his mother and later as a young man stealing saris from girls bathing in the river – and of the adventures of the epic *Mahabharata*.

Belur and Halebid

The most comfortable way to see these important Hoysala temples is to visit them on either side of an overnight stay at Hassan, 120km (75 miles) northwest of Mysore.

The **Chenna Kesava Temple** in **Belur** is also dedicated to Vishnu the Radiant, but it was built in 1117, 150 years before the Kesava at Somnathpur. Legend has it, however, that all Belur, Halebid and Somnathpur temples were designed by the same architect. The Belur temple's silhouette makes for an unfinished look, but it is not certain that towers or domes were ever planned. Here too, it is the sculpture rather than the form that gives the temple its impact.

The friezes bring the building to life with the legends of the gods, Shiva the demon-killer, or scenes from the *Mahabharata* including Prince Arjuna shooting a fish while looking at its reflection in an adjacent bowl of water. The bracket figures are masterpieces: a huntress, girls dancing or singing, and a woman about to spray her lover with rosewater. By the south doorway, on a vine chiselled beside the head of a girl dancing with a demon, you can find a lizard hunting a fly.

The **Hoysalesvara Temple** in **Halebid**, 16km (10 miles) from Belur, dedicated to Shiva and his wife Parvati, is the biggest of the Hoysala shrines. It suffered some destruction at the hands of Muslim iconoclasts, so it's worth visiting the **Archaeological Museum**, too, where some of the best of its statues are now kept. Look at

Sunflowers and coconuts near Halebid

the surprisingly fine carving of the bracket figures in the dancing hall, achieved by the craftsmen working with soft steatite soapstone which subsequently hardened to the texture of granite.

Sravanabelagola

Fifty kilometres (30 miles) east of Hassan, the Vindhyagiri Hill rises 140 metres (463ft) above the plateau, with one of the most dramatic monuments in all India, the statue of **Gommatesvara**, on its top. To get to it, you must climb barefoot – the hill is holy ground – up 644 steps cut in the rock. Take it easy, and you will find the trip well worthwhile.

Erected in AD 983, the statue crowns a sanctuary erected in the village of Sravanabelagola 1,400 years earlier by the Digambara sect of Jains, who regarded nakedness as part of the abnegation necessary to achieve true enlightenment. It is believed that in the 4th century BC, Chandragupta converted to Jainism at Sravanabelagola and fasted to death.

Statue of Gommatesvara

Coming upon the statue at the top of the hill, even though you may have already seen it from a distance, is still an awe-inspiring experience. This Jain saint stands 17.5 metres (57ft) tall, and is carved from a granite monolith polished by centuries of libations with milk.

Gommatesvara, the son of the prophet Adinath, is entirely naked except for a single vine-creeper winding itself around his legs and arms. The creeper symbolises the impassiveness he is said to have observed in this upright position of *pratimayoga*, which he adopted for one whole year in response to his brother's lust for worldly power. An anthill and serpents at his feet symbolise the mental agony that his smile shows he had conquered.

Hampi ㉓

Getting to Hampi

As well as being accessible from Bangalore, Hampi can also be reached from Goa by rail to the town of Hospet, half an hour from the ruins. The line running inland across the Western Ghats is now served by express trains, and the trip takes 8–9 hours.

It was among the huge boulder-strewn landscape of the Deccan plateau that a pair of brothers, Harihara and Bukka, escaped the clutches of the tyrannical Delhi Tuqhluq sultans sometime in the first half of the 14th century and carved out for themselves an independent kingdom. Within 150 years, the rule of the dynasty they founded extended from coast to coast and to the tip of India. Vast riches poured in from the trade in horses and spices across the Arabian Sea, which successive rulers lavished on carved temples, palaces and a glorious city spread around the bend in the sacred **Tungabadhra River**.

The empire's unifying force was its rulers' fear of attack from the north by the Deccani sultans. With its vast standing army, Hindu Vijayanagar was a major obstacle to the Muslim kingdoms' territorial ambitions, so it was inevitable that sooner or later the two would come into conflict. The decisive battle took place in 1565 at Talikota, in the no-man's-land buffering the warring kingdoms, and ended with the total destruction of the Vijayanagaran forces.

The ensuing sack of Vijayanagar lasted six months. By the end of it, the city whose grandeur had so impressed the Portuguese chronicler Domingo Paes in 1520 lay entirely in ruins, its inhabitants slaughtered, its temples, palaces and gardens burned to the ground and broken. Hindu pilgrims still come here to bathe in the river and worship at the Virupaksha shrine, whose gateway

Hampi

gopuras somehow survived the Muslim onslaught and still tower over the surrounding banana groves, visible for kilometres. For foreign visitors, the chief attractions of Hampi, aside from the wonderful archaeological remains, are the magical riverine landscape and surreal beauty of the boulder hills, which provide an exotic backdrop for bicycle rides and sunset walks around the ruins.

Visiting Hampi

Most visitors stay in the town of **Hospet**, 13km (8 miles) southwest of Hampi, which has a better choice of hotels and restaurants. From there it takes around half an hour to reach Hampi bazaar, whose western end is overwhelmed by the huge towers of the **Virupaksha Temple**. Follow the path leading from here along the riverside to the northern group of ruins, centred on the ornately carved **Vitthala Temple**. This is where you will see the finest examples of Vijayanagar's trademark 'rearing horse' columns.

You'll need to jump in a taxi to reach the southern, or 'Royal', group of monuments. En route, be sure to pull over half way to see the statue of Narashima – the huge, bulging-eyed depiction of Vishnu in his incarnation as the Man-Lion – that stands just off the roadside. Scattered over a wide area, the **Royal group**, a sprawling complex of palaces and ceremonial buildings, holds enough to keep interested visitors busy for days; in reality, the fierce Deccan heat is likely to limit how much you can take in at one go. Start at the

Mahanavami Dibba, a massive pyramidal platform erected to commemorate a victorious military campaign; its sides, and those of the nearby Kings' Audience Hall, are carved with rampaging elephants and mythological scenes. From there, work your way southeast towards the **Lotus Mahal**, where the queens and members of the *zenana* (harem) could relax in the shade of ornamental pavilions and domed corridors.

Finds from the archaeological site, including weapons, sculpture and palm-leaf manuscripts, are displayed at the **ASI museum** just south of the Royal group, alongside a scale model of medieval Vijayanagar which conveys just how vast and sophisticated the city was.

Bijapur ㉔

The powerful Bahmani dynasty formed the backbone of the Muslim military alliance that ultimately defeated Vijayanagar. This victory, and violent sack in 1565, provided the funds to endow their capital at **Bijapur**, northeast of Hampi, with a glittering crop of mosques, palaces and fortifications – collectively the finest display of Islamic architecture south of Agra.

Rising from the eastern fringes of town, Bijapur's *pièce de résistance* is the gigantic **Golgumbaz mausoleum**. The tomb dates from the twilight years of Bahmani rule and perfectly captures the spirit of a regime in decline: conceived on a ruinously grand scale, it exudes more self-importance than grace. All the same, it is an undeniably impressive spectacle. Capping the building, the vast freestanding dome is said to be the largest in the world after St Peter's in Rome.

The famous stone chariot at Hampi

Golconda Fort near Hyderabad

At the opposite end of town – and architectural spectrum – is the **Ibrahim Rauza**, a gem of a walled tomb built on an altogether more human scale. Its appeal lies in its ornate decor, notably the famous pierced stone *jali* windows cut in the form of Qu'ranic inscriptions, and slender minarets and cupolas, which provide cover for flocks of screeching parakeets.

Finally, on your way to the Ibrahim Rauza, a monument worth the short detour from Bijapur's western gateway is the **Malik-i-Maidan** ('Lord of the Plains'), a huge canon installed in the 16th century. It took 10 elephants, 1,000 bullocks and an army of men to haul it into place. Steps from the emplacement lead to a higher bastion from where you can enjoy a wonderful panoramic view over the town and surrounding countryside.

Hyderabad and Golconda

Hyderabad, capital of Andhra Pradesh, is India's fourth-largest city (pop. 6.8 million). It dates from 1591, when Mohammed Quli of the Qutb Shahi dynasty moved his capital here from nearby Golconda. In 1687 the Mughal Emperor Aurangzeb overthrew the dynasty and appointed a viceroy, whose descendants ruled as the Nizams of Hyderabad until 1949. For centuries renowned as one of Asia's wealthiest hubs due to its lucrative monopoly over the world's diamond supply, the state capital is today among India's industrial boom centres, with a rapidly expanding biochemical and biotech sector. The vast Hyderabad Information Technology Engineering Consultancy City (HITECC for short) on the outskirts accommodates the regional head offices of numerous international software giants, including Oracle and Microsoft.

The city's most famous landmark, however, is the 1591 **Charminar** ('four towers'), a magnificent square archway supported by four 56-metre (184ft) towers. Nearby stands one of the largest mosques in India, the black granite **Mecca Masjid**, said to have bricks made of red clay from Mecca over the central archway. Surrounding the Charminar are bazaars with narrow cobbled lanes lined with rows of shops selling spices, tobacco, grain, perfume oils and Hyderabadi specialities. There is also a pearl market.

Golconda Fort

A visit to the former capital of the Qutb Shahi dynasty, **Golconda Fort**, 11km (7 miles) west of Hyderabad, is an easy day-trip via local bus or auto-rickshaw. It was used by the last of the Qutb kings in the 17th century as a bastion against Mughal attack. Situated on a steep hill, the fort was encircled by immense walls with 87 semicircular bastions and eight gates with elephant-proof spikes. The remains of its once splendid palaces and gardens give an idea of its former grandeur. Diamonds and rubies once embellished the walls of the Queen's Palace, and rose-water filled a copper fountain.

Tirupati

In the south of Andhra Pradesh, Tirupati, with nearby Tirumala Hill on which stands the Lord Venkatesvara Temple, is the busiest pilgrimage site in the world, as well as one of the wealthiest. The very efficient temple administration employs around 16,000 people to deal with the 60,000-plus pilgrims a day who come for darshan (a view of the god). Many of them shave their heads as a pledge, or to thank the deity. The hair is used to make wigs, which are sold locally and exported. The temple is open to non-Hindus, but they must sign a form declaring their faith in god and respect for the temple's procedures. The steep road up the hill, with 57 hairpin bends, is not for the faint-hearted.

WHAT TO DO

SPORTS

One thing the Indians enjoyed about the British was their enthusiasm for sports – hockey and cricket in particular. In return, the British learned the delights of polo (imported with the Mughals from Persia and Afghanistan). Today, sporting life in India is still very active. Delhi especially has very modern facilities, created to host the 2010 Commonwealth Games.

Outdoor Activities

Be careful to adapt your activities to the climate, and avoid going out in the midday sun.

Swimming. Many luxury hotels have swimming pools, but for health reasons, avoid swimming in rivers, ponds, lakes and reservoirs. Beach swimming is best at the recognised resorts rather than at the major ports. In Mumbai, for instance, both Juhu and Chowpatty beaches are definitely a bad idea, and though the Marina beaches in Chennai are cleaner, there is a deadly undertow. The best resort beaches are on the west coast in Kerala and Goa. On the east coast, try Gopalpur-on-Sea on the south of Odisha, or the beaches north of Puducherry, in Tamil Nadu.

Watersports. Goa is the place to go for more adventurous activities, with kite-surfing and parascending on offer. In the Lakshadweep archipelago off the Keralan coast, and the Andaman Islands, two-hours' flight east of Chennai, the snorkelling and diving are superb.

Wildlife. India has 70 or so national parks and 330-plus sanctuaries. Among the most famous are Corbett, Kanha and Ranthambore national parks (for tigers), Gir Forest (for Asiatic lions), Periyar Wildlife Sanctuary (for elephants) and Eravikulam National Park

Brightly painted Theyyam dancer, Kerala

(for the endangered Nilgiri Tahr, a type of ibex) and Kaziranga (for its rare one-horned rhino).

Hiking. Trekking, as it is most often called here, is a marvellous way of getting away from the often madding crowd in India, and you will find it is well organised in the regions of Ladakh, the Kullu Valley (Himachal Pradesh) and Garhwal (Uttarkhand). Other trekking hot spots in the east include Sikkim, where you can walk to Kanchenjunga Base Camp. In the country's southwest, the hill stations of the Western Ghats near the Kerala-Tamil Nadu border are good bases for shorter treks.

Travel agencies happily provide a range of camping and cooking equipment, as well as the guides, cooks and porters you need, and a jeep for travelling to more remote and inaccessible areas. The

A Passion for Cricket

Wherever you go in India, you'll see groups of youngsters engaged in a game of cricket. The Indians are passionate about the sport, and they play it wherever they can: in the backstreets, on the beaches, in the parks; in fact on any piece of flat ground where cricket could be played. Their knock-about games are keenly contested, and whether bowlers or batters, budding street talents have always wanted to emulate their heroes in the national side: heroes of the past, like Gundappa Viswanath, Kapil Dev and Sunil Gavaskar; and those of the present, like Sachin Tendulkar, Virender Sehwag, Cheteshwar Pujara and Mahendra Dhoni. There is little chance of talent being recognised in the streets, however. Most cricketers who end up playing at the top level have much more privileged backgounds, coming from the wealthy, educated élite.

The Indians share their love of cricket with their neighbours, the Pakistanis, and sporting encounters between these giants of the game have always engendered the most passionate emotions of all. Amid the thaw in relations between the two countries, the rivalry on the pitch has helped cement friendships off it, and cricket, as well as being the national passion, has worked diplomatic wonders.

necessary arrangements can easily be seen to on the spot, but a more ambitious six-or seven-day trek needs some notice, so it would be best to book with your travel agent and settle the details before you leave home. A quick search on the Internet will reveal dozens of Himalayan trekking specialists.

Spectator Sports

Cricket. The most beloved sport in India by far. There is something in the intricacy of its arcane rules and controlled passion that appeals to the Indian people. It is an astounding obsession, and all major cities have stadiums. The most fervent atmosphere of all can

Cricket is a national passion

be experienced at the Eden Gardens Stadium, home of the Kolkata Cricket Club, founded in 1792, just five years after the Marylebone Cricket Club in London. The new wham-bam Twenty20 format is particularly popular, and has been given a massive boost by the 2008 launch of the multi-million-dollar Indian Premier League (www.iplt20.com), showcasing a range of top international cricketing stars.

Hockey is a British import, in which the Indians have surpassed their former masters. Today they often share the Olympic finals with their old arch-rivals, Pakistan.

Polo is a Rajasthani speciality, but tournaments are also held in Delhi and Mumbai during the winter months. This is a rich man's sport, particularly popular in the Rajasthani capital, Japiur, where it's also, uniquely, played with elephants.

Traditional dancers in action

Horse racing is popular, with races such as the Kolkata Derby, St. Leger, and the Oaks in Mumbai. The highest course in the country is at Darjeeling. Camel racing is a big event at Jaisalmer's Desert Festival in January/February and also at the Camel Fair at Pushkar.

ENTERTAINMENT

Film

Film in India, produced mainly in the cities of Chennai, Mumbai and Kolkata, is a major industry. The large-scale production of entertainment films is a cultural phenomenon. You may well be more baffled by the appeal of the colourful musical comedies and violent shoot-em-ups than you would be in the West, but the emotion of the melodramas and romantic adventure stories of India's cultural and historic past have considerable curiosity value for a rainy afternoon. If you watch the action closely, you can learn a lot about Indian people by what makes them cheer, laugh or weep. Kolkata and Thiruvananthapuram seem to be the only production centres having any pretensions to art cinema at all, but ironically you're actually more likely to see the works of Satyajit Ray or Mrinal Sen shown in Europe or North America than in India itself.

Music

Music of South Asia differs between the north and south, urban and rural environments, and men and women. The music most commonly associated with India in the West is that of the North Indian concert stage (known generally as **Hindustani** music), whose genres have their roots in the Muslim courts. However, South India has its own concert traditions (known as **Karnatic** music), in part stemming from the music of the southern courts, but also owing a great deal to a strong tradition of devotional song.

The concert music of South Asia uses a basic collection of seven pitches *(svara)* within an octave – *sa, ri, ga, ma, pa, dha, ni, (sa)* – which roughly correspond to the doh, re, mi etc. of Western music,

Film music

The Indian music with the largest audience is *filmi git* (film song). The first Indian 'talkie', *Alam Ara*, was made in Mumbai in 1931. Following the conventions of traditional theatre, the action was broken up by songs and dances that served to push the action forward and represented the passing of time. These early films gained great popularity, and so did the songs.

The singers in the early films were the actors and actresses themselves, but when recording technology allowed the songs to be dubbed in the late 1930s, most songs became pre-recorded, and specialists, known as playback-singers, took over. By this time, film song had become phenomenally popular, and playback singers became musical superstars.

The most popular, and enduring, of all playback-singers is Lata Mangeshkar. She, her sister Asha Bhosle, and singers such as Geeta Dutt, perform in a high-pitched style, very different to the lower, richer voices of the singers of the 1930s, and this has now become the dominant female film music vocal style. Popular male singers include Mohammad Rafi and Mukesh.

Musician Rama Varma, playing the vina

and also have upper and lower ('sharp' and 'flat') variants. However, they differ radically from Western pitches by not having a fixed value; for example, *sa* is fixed at a convenient level (higher or lower) for each individual musician, to suit an instrument, or his or her voice. Also essential to both Hindustani and Karnatic music are the twin concepts of *raga* and *tala*.

Raga (Sanskrit 'colour') designates which pitches it is permissible to play during the performance of a piece, and also characteristic phrases, 'ornamentations' as well as – although this is now less common – the time of day at which individual *ragas* should be played. This is particularly true of north India; in the south, concepts of *raga* tend to rely much more on the classification of different collections of pitches. Often misrepresented as merely a 'scale' or 'mode', a *raga* is more than a lineally arranged group of pitches (although this is often the most convenient way of notating them), but also implies the approach the musician should take towards the *svara*.

Tala (Sanskrit 'clapping') is the name for the repeating rhythmic cycles that underpin the metred sections of any Hindustani or

Karnatic performance. Different *talas* consist of different numbers of beats (matra), and the first beat of a cycle, known in the north as *sam*, provides a reference point, not only for the musicians, but also the audience. At a performance of Karnatak music it is common to see the audience collectively marking the cycle through claps and waves on strong and weak beats respectively.

Khayal is the Hindustani vocal genre most often heard in the concert hall. A *khayal* composition (*bandis* or *ciz*) comprises two short sections, known as *sthayi* and *antara*, in contrasting registers. Usually two compositions are presented, the first in a slow tempo, known as a 'big' (*bara*) *khayal*, the second, a 'small' (*chota*) *khayal* in a faster tempo, which speeds up towards the end of the performance.

A *khayal* concert starts with a short unmetred section introducing the *raga* (mode or pitch collection), followed by the *ciz*, which is in *tala* (rhythmic cycle), the most common of which is the 16-beat *tintal*. It is accompanied by the *tabla* (paired kettledrums) and, traditionally, the bowed lute, *sarangi* (this is now usually replaced by the harmonium, a small hand-pumped organ that was introduced to South Asian music by French missionaries). The drone-lute *tambura* provides a constant background; it is sometimes played by a supporting singer and usually tuned to *sa* and *pa* (roughly corresponding to the Western doh and soh). The compositions are explored in a series of elaborations and improvisations.

Although sharing similar basic concepts of *raga*, *tala* and *svara*, Karnatic music differs from the concert music of the north, perhaps most evidently in its performance of fully composed pieces, a lesser degree of improvisation and an important tradition of devotional song. Also, Karnatic music has tended to be a Brahmanical tradition, as opposed to that of either the Muslim or lower-caste musicians of the north. Karnatic music is overwhelmingly oriented towards vocal performance, especially with its emphasis on devotional texts. Vocal forms often included in concerts include the *kriti*, *varnam*, *kirtana* and *ragam-tanam-pallavi*. The latter form, in contrast to the devotional *kirtana* and *kriti*, stems from the musical traditions of the south Indian courts and is considered a great technical skill.

Local performance traditions in India are usually associated with life-cycle and calendrical rituals, and also village festivals, often for local deities. Births, deaths and weddings are all accompanied by music, particularly by women singing. Marriage processions are usually accompanied by bands, traditionally playing oboes and drums, but now more commonly by brass bands playing covers of film songs. Funerals have traditionally been accompanied by low-caste drummers. Music and dance also accompany festivals such as Holi and the yearly Ganapati puja. At other times people gather in temples to collectively sing *bhajan* (devotional songs).

In south Indian temples, processions of the deities are accompanied by the *periya melam* ensemble of *nagasvaram* (oboe) and *tavil* (barrel drum).

Nightlife

Mumbai, with its more relaxed attitudes to alcohol, is home to India's most legendary nightlife. Frequented by Bollywood stars and the

A Bollywood film poster

city's mega rich set, the hippest clubs, such as Blue Frog (www.bluefrog.co.in), Aer Bar in the Four Seasons Hotel (www.fourseasons.com) and Enigma at the JW Marriott are these days in, or within easy reach of, the affluent central and northern suburbs. In Delhi, Connaught Place has a good number of watering holes, and the Elevate club on the top floor of Centre Stage Mall is a great venue. Goa's infamous beach parties are not what they once were, but Tito's in Baga, Westend at Calangute, Club Cubana in Arpora and Club

Bright silks

Fresh in Aswem enjoy an international reputation and host mega parties over Christmas and New Year.

SHOPPING

From the Greeks to the Turks and Mughals, from Marco Polo to Lord Mountbatten, all have been seduced by India's riches. It is still a great place to shop.

Traditional craftwork continues to be produced at the highest level of skill: silks, carpets, jewellery, perfumes, brassware and woodcarving are first class, and you will have the added bonus of dealing with the most charming bunch of merchants in the world.

At least half the pleasure is in the bargaining. If you don't want to be fleeced, don't plunge in blindly. Go first to the Government Cottage Industry Emporiums, which can be found in almost every major city. The selection here is not usually as wide as you'll find in the privately run shops and you can't haggle, but it will give you an idea of the range of goods, the quality and, above all, the correct price.

Then you're ready for the fray, either in the bustling great bazaars such as Delhi's Chandni Chowk or Mumbai's Bhuleshwar, or the more sedate ambience of grander shops and showrooms. The one street market you shouldn't miss is Mumbai's Chor Bazaar, or Thieves' Market, which is an extravagant flea market where, among other things, you'll see Indian motorists buying back spare parts stolen from their cars the night before, or so the urban myth goes; the market is actually more famous for repro/fake antiques.

If, during your tours of the big cities, you come across products you like from places you will be visiting later, such as Rajasthan, Varanasi or Kashmir, wait until you get there – the price and selection may be much better.

Haggling with dapper Gujaratis and the bright-eyed Kashmiris can attain the level of high art. Even if you don't land a bargain, there is real aesthetic pleasure in seeing, at the end of the verbal 'combat', the disarray of silks thrown across a counter or a mound of carpets on the floor. Fleeing the insurgency war and dearth of tourists in their homeland, Kashmiri handicraft vendors have fanned out to tourist centres across India. Carpets and papier mâché are their traditional wares, but they also sell artefacts made by Tibetan refugees.

If there is no magic formula for the perfect bargain – each person will have his or her own psychological approach – you should avoid two extremes: don't be too eager, and don't, on the other hand, assume everybody is out to cheat you. It spoils the sport.

Art. For modern painting, try the art galleries around Connaught Place in New Delhi and Mumbai's Jehangir Gallery, not to forget the Academy of Fine Arts in Kolkata.

Carpets. Ever since the days when the Mughal Emperor Jahangir took Persian craftsmen up to Kashmir with him during his long summer holidays, the handwoven silk-and-woollen carpets of Srinagar have been among the best in the world and are one of the most attractive purchases you can make. The silk gives the carpets their unique sheen. The prices will vary according to the proportions of silk and wool used and the density of the weave itself; naturally, none of these pieces are cheap.

A sari shop

Look out for traditional Persian and original Kashmiri motifs such as peacocks and fruit trees, tiger hunts, and Mughal lovers. Indeed many of the carpets seem just too lovely to walk on, but they make superb wall hangings, and even if you can't remortgage your house to buy a big one, a modest bedside rug can do wonders to warm and brighten a room.

Cottons. Either hand-printed or embroidered, cottons are probably the best bargain of all Indian textiles, made into tablecloths, napkins, bed linen, spreads, pillowcases and airy, light scarves that make life much more comfortable in the Indian heat. Indian tailors are cheap, good and fast, so you might consider having lightweight shirts and baggy pants made up for you during your stay.

Three cotton prints to look out for, particularly in Rajasthan, are: *bagru*, consisting of geometric or fish, almond and vine patterns in blue, brown and maroon; *sanganeri*, block printed floral and paisley patterns; and *bandhani*, tie-dye, which results in decorative colour. The bright motifs with mirror-work stitched into them, much favoured by Rajasthani women of the desert for their long flowing skirts, are known as *kutchi* or *saurashtra*. The dashing, rather coarse cotton Punjabi *phulkari* shawls are made from fabric with patterns in orange, pink, green, red and yellow.

Jewellery. Whether made with precious or semi-precious stones, jewellery is important in India. The jewellery of Rajasthan is much sought after. Indian diamond mines produced some of the world's greatest gems, including the Koh-i-noor (Mountain of Light), now in the British crown jewels, having originally been set in the Peacock Throne. Although the mines have been superseded by those in South America and South Africa, the art of cutting and polishing still continues in Surat, Gujarat.

However, the essential pieces of jewellery in India are the bangle and the simple golden chain necklace. Whole stalls are devoted to bangles, made from silver and gold, metal, wood, glass, plastic and – best bargain of all – colourful varnished papiermâché from Kashmir.

Metals. Gold, silver, copper and brass – each has its own bazaar in the big neighbourhood markets of Delhi, Mumbai and Kolkata. Of these, the best known is Jains' Zaveri Bazaar in Mumbai, where antique gold is sold.

Shawls. Cashmere, often in the form of 'pashmina', is a shawl of soft, warm wool shorn, you will be told, from the underbelly of the wild Himalayan sheep. 'Shahtoosh' is the finest Kashmir wool of all, taken from the throat of the ibex and woven so finely that one can pass a shawl right through a wedding ring. These are expensive, but you can get shawls of good quality wool with distinctive embroidery at more reasonable prices.

Beautifully decorated shoes on sale in Delhi

Silks. Having long been basic to a fine Indian woman's wardrobe, silks also make magnificent

Shopping for bangles

tunics, blouses, stoles or long scarves for a Western outfit. The costume more easily adapted to Western tastes than the sari, perhaps because it involves trousers, is a long tunic worn over baggy pantaloons with a stole around the shoulders; known as salwar kameez, it is most ubiquitous in the northwest.

Three towns are famous for their silk: Bengaluru, for its classic printed silk; Varanasi, for its gold and silver brocades; and Kanchipuram, for its heavy, brilliantly coloured silk, favoured for formal saris. Not forgetting the men, the city of Kanchipuram also produces superb silk ties.

Spices. Available in many markets around the country. If you want to take some home, it's best to buy them in their whole form, to preserve freshness. Tea enthusiasts will make a beeline for Darjeeling, to purchase directly from the plantations or at the town bazaar. When you take a couple of kilos, they'll ship it for you in airtight packages.

Wood carvings. A variety are on offer, from rosewood elephants or sandalwood camels to the Kashmiris' finely fretted walnut, created in the style of the screens on the Srinagar houseboats.

Festivals and fairs

In a country with such a strong and varied religious tradition, there is always some reason for celebrating something. Here is a selection (but note, the dates are moveable because India follows a lunar calendar; precise dates around the time of travel are available through any tourist office):

January: *Pongal*, in Tamil Nadu. A three-day harvest festival during which cows and bullocks are fed with rice, this is a celebration of the prosperity associated with the harvest. The atmosphere is generally jolly; the highlight is a variation on the bullfight in which young men try to pluck rupee notes from the horns of a very angry bull.

January 26: *Republic Day*, Delhi. Great march in which India shows off its cultural diversity and military might.

January/February: *Vasant Panchami*, throughout India but best seen in Kolkata. Honouring Sarasvati, goddess of scholars and artists; everyone dresses up in bright yellow and flies kites. *Desert Festival*, Jaisalmer. A lively celebration of Rajasthani music and dance, plus camel races in the local stadium.

February/March: *Carnival*, Goa. A hint of Portugal mixed with India; costumes and dancing in the streets. *Shivratri*, India-wide. Solemn celebration of Shiva, with all-night music and prayers in the temples. *Holi*, northern India, best at Mathura. The spring festival when Indians spray each other with coloured powder and water.

March/April: *Gangaur*, Rajasthan. Procession of girls balancing brilliantly polished brass pitchers on their heads with which they bathe Shiva's wife Parvati (Gauri); the garlanded deity is then accompanied by Shiva at the head of a parade of horses and elephants.

April/May: *Spring Festival*, Srinagar. Kashmiris bring out their samovars for a big tea party to celebrate the first almond blossoms, highlighted by mid-April festivities in the Mughal Gardens. *Baisakhi*, all over north India. The Hindus' solar New Year. The Sikhs celebrate the anniversary of Guru Gobind Singh's exhortation to form the *khalsa* ('army of the pure').

June/July: *Rath Yatra*, Puri. One of the greatest festivals of the year, when the three gigantic temple-chariots of Jagannath, his brother Balabhadra and sister Subhadra are drawn through the streets.

July/August: *Amarnath Yatra*, Kashmir. During the full moon, thousands of pilgrims make their way from Pahalgam to the cave of Amarnath to Shiva's ice-stalagmite lingam.

September/October: *Dussehra*, Mysore, Delhi and Kolkata. Ten days of pageant; elephant processions following behind the Maharaja of Mysore's throne; in north India, there is music, dance and drama centring in Delhi on the legendary hero Rama and in Kolkata on the goddess Durga.

October/November: *Pushkar Fair*. Camels, horses and bullocks are brought to market. *Diwali*, all over India. The Festival of Lights celebrating Rama and Sita's homecoming, as described in the *Ramayana*. *Kali Puja*, Bengal. Celebrations in honour of the goddess Kali, whose images are displayed on special pandals around the city, then bathed in the Hooghly River.

November: *Sonepur Cattle Fair*, near Patna. On the banks of the Ganges, this month-long cattle and elephant market is one of the world's biggest.

December 25: *Christmas*, Mumbai, Goa and Kerala. A more religious observance than in most Western countries.

Variable dates:
Muharram, Lucknow. Muslim mourning for Imam Hussein, grandson of Mohammed. Spectacular illuminated bamboo and paper replicas of the martyr's tomb are paraded through the town.
Eid-Al-Fitr, Lucknow, Delhi and Kolkata. Mosques are lit up as Muslims celebrate the end of the Ramadan fast.

EATING OUT

India's cuisine is as diverse and sophisticated as its civilisation. Every region of the country boasts its own distinctive specialities, reflecting the various climates and produce available, as well as cultural and historic influences. And you won't necessarily find the best local cooking in swanky five stars. Often, the most remarkable Indian cuisine is served at simple, inexpensive restaurants where discerning local office workers come for their lunch. That said, middle-class Indians, in particular, love to dine out in plush surroundings, and a wealth of possibilities are on offer in the big cities, where these days authentic Italian, Thai or Lebanese food are as easy to come by as sheesh kebab or chicken korma.

Dishes tend to be highly seasoned, but the spices are subtle; it will take some time for you to get used to the flavours, even if you're familiar with Indian cuisine back home. Don't be afraid to taste local dishes (provided they're served hygienically). It's unlikely that you came to India to eat the same food that you're used to back home. Other than in Goa, few hotels break the beef taboo to serve steaks or hamburgers, though you may find some made from buffalo meat.

Breakfast, coffee and tea

In large hotels and tourist resorts, typical Western breakfasts are usually available: from banana porridge to freshly baked pain au chocolat or muesli, served with tropical, fresh seasonal fruits such as papaya and pineapple, and their juices. Bread tends to be heavier and stodgier than back home due (India's wheat strains don't seem to quite hit the spot and imported ones cost a fortune), and many visitors end up ordering chapatis or rotis rather in favour of croissants and brown toast.

With the emerge of specialist chains such as Café Coffee Day and Starbucks, proper coffee from a real espresso machine is no longer the rarity it was a decade ago, at least in the cities and resorts; and down south you'll find a pleasant, if rather weak, filter variety made from locally grown beans. Modern, air-con coffee shops tend to cater for a predominantly young, urban elite who are looking for somewhere cool to hangout, conduct business meetings or simply escape the chaos outside. For middle-class women, desperately short of safe public spaces, coffee shops also provide a haven where they're not likely to be leered at. And the loos will be clean. In short, the rise of the modern Indian coffee shop is not really about the coffee – though it does mean you're never far from a decent cappuccino.

Tea is rarely Darjeeling or single-estate Assam. Regular Indian chai is instead made from low-grade 'crush-tear-and-curl' ('CTC') blends that produce a strong, dark brew and good caffeine hit. It's drunk milky and very sweet, in small cups. For safety's sake the milk (which usually comes from buffalo rather than cows) is boiled, then cooled for the cereals.

Making delicious snacks in Lucknow

The typical North Indian breakfast is a pile of hot *chapatis* or *parathas* with spicy fillings and a side portion of dhal along with cold set yoghurt. In the south, you'll find favourites *idlis* (steamed rice cakes) and *vadas* (fried doughnuts made of lentils), served with firey bowls of sambar broth and coconut *chatni*. Pongal, a kind of savoury porridge flavoured with mustard seeds and fresh green kari leaves, is also common.

Lunch and dinner

Hotels will often provide large buffets, giving you a chance to try several dishes, which people tend to pile up on one plate

Lentils and spices in the bazaar

around a large mound of rice. But traditional Indian meals are served on a *thali*, a large metal platter, with up to 10 dishes in separate little bowls, *katori*, so that you can savour the different tastes separately and work out which ones you particularly like. *Thalis* (or "meals" as they're known in the south) are very good value and often change on a daily basis.

Places that have assimilated the British custom will serve a soup like mulligatawny, which is a spicy chicken, mutton or vegetable broth created for colonial officials. Otherwise, with the exception of the food served at great banquets, meals are not divided into courses; everything will usually arrive on your thali at the same time.

You will find it beneficial to follow the Indian custom of drinking something either before or after, but not during, a meal. Drinking does not in the end alleviate a peppery flavour because it will leave your taste buds completely defenceless against the next hot mouthful. Therefore, it's better to eat some plain rice or one of the soft Indian bananas, or, best of all, yoghurt flavoured with mint. Yoghurt is known as curd and is eaten in both the north and the south for its cooling digestive properties.

Indians eat with their fingers, rotating the fingertips around the plate to form the food into a ball with rice or bread. Cutlery may be provided, but a fork is not necessarily any more hygienic than fingers.

'Curry'

Properly speaking, there is no such thing as a curry. It's a British term invented to refer indiscriminately to India's spicy preparations of fish, meat and vegetables. It probably derives from the *kari* leaf common in southern cooking; an alternative theory is that the term comes from the copper *karai* dishes in which Mughal cookery is traditionally served.

In India there is not one 'curry powder' or 'curry sauce', because each dish has its own spices. The combination commonly used in a basic mixture of sautéed onions and garlic is called *garam masala*, a powdered blend of coriander, cumin, ginger, black pepper, cinnamon, chilli, cardamom, bay leaves, cloves and nutmeg. Saffron adds its own unique colour and fragrance, both to rice and to meat.

Non-vegetarian

The classical cuisine of the north, *mughlai*, comes from the Mughals. With beef taboo for Hindus and pork for Muslims, the meat is chicken, lamb or mutton, its classic 'curry' being *rogan josh*. Cubes of meat are prepared in a yogurt sauce made with chilli, ginger, coriander and garam masala. This dish originated in Kashmir, where they eat lamb in dozens of different ways (if you attend a *wazwan* banquet, there may be as many as 16, 36 or even 52 dishes).

Other dishes are the *kebab*, balls of lamb minced with almond and spices; *tabakmas*, mutton ribs with a crispy skin; and *goshtaba*, the most tender lamb from the breast, with every last sinew beaten out of it before it is minced into a fragrant dumpling stewed in

Spices and health

You may be pleased to know that, according to the ancient canons of Indian medicine, the myriad spices in your meal are all working to improve your health. While the combination stimulates the appetite and helps your digestion in this very special climate, some of the individual spices have surprising properties.

Turmeric is very good for skin ailments, ginger for your liver and rheumatism. Cloves can help the kidneys, relieve fever and also stimulate the heart. Coriander fights constipation and insomnia, but one of the most versatile is cardamom, battling bad breath, headaches, throaty coughs and haemorrhoids.

yoghurt. In Kashmir this is the climactic dish of a wedding banquet after eating the liver, the kidneys, the shoulder, the leg and various minced kebabs.

Biryani is a Mughlai speciality, originally exclusively a lamb dish, though chicken, fish and vegetables are now cooked in the same way. This dish is more elaborate than *pulao*, which is a simple mixture of rice and lightly flavoured meat or vegetables. Biryani is chicken or lamb cooked in a sauce of ginger, cardamom, cinnamon and cloves, before steaming it with saffron rice and *ghee* (clarified butter). It may be served decorated with almonds, mint and slices of boiled egg.

Chickens tend to be scrawny, but they are tasty in a creamy *makhani* butter sauce as *murg ilaychi*, marinated in yoghurt with cardamom, ginger, peppers and saffron, or *murg do pyaza*, with onions. *Tandoori* chicken is a popular barbecue in the northwest style, baked in a *tandoor* clay oven. Typically, the chicken is salted and doused in lime juice, tenderised with papaya, then marinated

Making chapatis

in yogurt with a flavouring of ginger, garlic, chilli and saffron, before being plunged on a spit into the charcoal-heated oven.

Fish and giant prawns, marinated in different sauces, also make very good tandoori dishes. Fresh seafood is widely available, particularly from the kitchens of Goa.

Rice and chapatis

The best rice is the aromatic

Ultra-vegetarianism

India's strictest vegetarians exclude fish, meat, poultry and eggs, and even blood-coloured vegetables such as beetroot or tomato, quoting the ancient Sanskrit verse: 'In the next world animals will eat those who eat them in this world'. Some Brahmins of Bengal do eat fish, calling them 'fruit of the sea'.

long-grained basmati, the common or garden variety known as *patna*. Apart from biryani and pulao, north Indian cuisine does not feature large quantities of rice as does south Indian cuisine. The Indians in the north prefer to eat their food with a variety of breads, including a floppy, thin *roti* or *chapati*; a slightly thicker *paratha*, sometimes stuffed with vegetables or minced meat; small deep-fried *puri*; or giant puffed-up *nan*, baked in a tandoor. Here's a tip: before you tackle the rice dishes of the south, try eating with your fingers in the north by folding a piece of roti around each morsel.

Vegetarian

Favourite vegetable dishes, or *sabzi*, are *aloo gobi* (cauliflower and potato), *bhaingan bharta* (roasted eggplant), *saag panir* (spinach with Indian soft cheese), *bhindi* (okra, aka 'ladies' fingers'), *channa* (chick-peas) and *dal* (lentils).

The cuisine of southern India is more vegetarian than that of the north. This is because the region was not subject to the Mughal influence. Whereas the north cooks with the products of its cattle, such as ghee for frying, yoghurt for sauces, and milk for desserts, the basis of southern cooking is the coconut – its oil is used for frying, and the milk and flesh for sauces. This gives the food a sweeter taste than in other regions. Sauces, in which water, palm vinegar or coconut milk is added to the spices, are gradually absorbed by the rice as the meal progresses.

Side dishes and snacks

Salads don't exist in the Western sense, but *cachumbar* is a refreshing side dish of tomato and onion seasoned with fresh lime juice, coriander leaves or vinegar. The great palate-cooler, eaten both in the north and south, is *raita*, a mixture of cold seasoned yoghurt and either cucumbers, tomatoes or pineapples.

As a sweet condiment, Indians serve not only mango, but mint and coconut, fresh ginger, tomato, dates or even tamarind in a spicy *chatni*. You'll find that some of the flavours in these dishes pack an astonishing double punch of sweet and sharp.

There are some wonderfully tangy Indian snacks. Mumbai's best is the *bhelpuri* sold on Chowpatty Beach (see page 134), a spicy snack made from fried puffed rice, flavoured with tamarind

Goa for gourmets

This former Portuguese colony, with a large Christian community, holds a unique position on the country's gastronomic map. Happy to use pork and beef in its very spicy 'curries' and pungent sausages, Goans also makes splendid use of the abundant seafood available off the Malabar coast.

Tisryo is a delicate dish of tiny stewed clams, spiced with ginger and sprinkled with coconut. But Goa's most celebrated dish, the 'Goan curry', is a thick sauce of tamarind, coconut, onions and tomatoes, served over a variety of local seafood such as clams, prawns, crab and anything else the fishermen have caught that day, all of it spiced to the gills. Known in English simply as 'fish curry', it's eaten twice each day by working Goans. You probably won't have room for an *alebele*, a sweet and spicy crêpe stuffed with coconut. But if you do, eat it with with *feni*, a potent spirit distilled from either cashew fruit juice or partly fermented palm sap.

juice, chillies and other spices. *Samosas* are stuffed with meat or vegetables, and *pakora* is a vegetable fritter. *Pani puri* is a small pastry stuffed with spiced tamarind water: put the whole thing in your mouth at once.

Desserts

Ras malai are delicious patties made from cottage cheese and nuts, sweetened with aromatic syrup, and perfumed with rose water and cardamom. *Khir*, rice

Cashews and feni in Goa

pudding, invented in India with condensed milk and broken rice, mixed with cardamom and nuts, is far superior to its British counterpart. *Gajar halwa*, a dessert of grated carrots stewed in milk and syrup, is best hot, with raisins and nuts. *Kulfi* is ice cream made with cardamom and pistachio. *Barfi* and *halwa* are sweets made with flour or milk and flavoured with nuts and cardamom.

Drinks

Tea – or *chai* – is India's national drink and is drunk strong, milky and sweet in tiny cups or glasses. The most cooling drinks are *nimbu pani* (water with fresh lime); fruit juices, especially from the fragrant Kashmiri apple; and *lassi*, a yoghurt-based sweet or salty drink that is refreshing but can take some getting used to, especially in its salty form.

Attitudes to alcohol vary across India, with Mumbai and Delhi the most liberal. Indian beers (Goa's Kingfisher is one of the best) and wines (produced in the hills outside Bombay and Pune) are certainly drinkable. Imported New World wines are very expensive and, frankly, not good to drink with Indian food anyway. Among traditional Indian alcoholic drinks are palm toddy in Kerala; *chang*, a barley beer from Ladakh; and *feni* in Goa.

Street food in Old Delhi

TO HELP YOU READ THE MENU

aloo potato

barfi sugar and milk sweets

biryani slow-cooked north Indian rice and meat dish

chai tea

chapatti unleavened bread cooked on a pan or griddle

chawal rice

dal lentils

faluda vermicelli with milk and ice cream

ghee clarified butter

ghosht meat, generally mutton

gulab jamun deep-fried dough balls soaked in syrup

halwa carrot- or semolina-based dessert

idli little dumpling of steamed rice flour, eaten at breakfast
with chutney and curry

jhinga prawns

kebab barbecued meat

keema minced meat, generally mutton

kofta spicy minced-meat balls

korma a curd-based curry sauce

kulfi Indian ice cream

lassi yoghurt-based milkshake, sweet or salty

macchli fish

makhan butter

masala mixed spices

masala dosa pancake of rice flour and ground lentils with spicy potato filling

murg chicken

mutter peas

nan leavened bread

nimbu pani fresh lime with water

nimbu soda fresh lime with soda

pakora deep-fried savory fritter with onion or potato

paneer Indian cottage cheese

papadum crispy spicy wafers

paratha flaky chapati, generally fried in butter and often stuffed

piaza onion

pomfret type of very fleshy fish

pulao north Indian rice and meat dish

puri deep-fried 'bubble' chapati

raita yoghurt (*dahi*) mixed with either tomatoes, green peppers, cucumbers, potatoes or pineapple

roomali roti paper-thin chapati

roti generic name for oven- or pan-cooked bread

sabzi vegetables

sag spinach

samosa deep-fried, stuffed pasties

seer type of white fish

tandoori meat (generally chicken) marinated in spice and yoghurt, cooked in a traditional oven

tikka pieces of diced meat/fish, marinated and grilled

A–Z TRAVEL TIPS

A Summary of Practical Information

A

ACCOMMODATION

Indian tourist accommodation caters to all tastes. Luxury hotels can be found in big cities and tourist centres and converted maharajas' palaces in former princely states. Other heritage properties in former colonial centres, such Goa, Puducherry, Cochin and Kolkata are run by large companies or descendants of their original owners. Further forms of accommodation unique to India include the floating houseboat hotels of Srignagar's Dal Lake, Kerala's converted *kettuvallam* rice barges, former British tea planters' bungalows in the Nilgiri and Cardamom Hills of the far south, Rajasthani-style desert camps in maharajas' hunting tents, and state-of-the-art eco lodges in remote forests and wildlife reserves. In the humid forests lining the Tamil Nadu-Kerala border, you can even spend the night in a jungle canopy tree house. B&Bs, known in India as 'homestays' are increasingly popular in some states, particularly Rajasthan and Ladakh (book through the relevant tourist office). The majority of Indian hotels, however, are bland, western-style places, offering a range of differently priced accommodation. There's generally a choice of AC and non-AC (air-con). The latter tend to be higher up the building, and larger. Soundproofing is not always adequate, and overhead fans and AC units may be noisy, so always keep ear plugs handy. Be wary of the water in the plastic flask near your bed. In the cheaper hotels, check your bed linen and do not hesitate to have it changed if necessary.

In popular tourist areas such as Rajasthan, Kerala and Goa, you'll find great variation in room tariffs across the year. High season starts in mid-December, peaks around Christmas and New Year, and ends in mid-January. At this time you'll need to book well in advance and expect inflated rates. In all resorts other than the hill stations (such as Shimla and Manali), low season means the monsoon period, when you can usually pick from plenty of bargains – especially in the beach resorts.

AIRPORTS

Indira Gandhi International Airport (DEL; tel: 0124-337 6000; www.newdelhiairport.in), New Delhi, is located 20km (12 miles) southwest of the city. The best way into the centre is via the Delhi Airport Metro Express line (www.delhiairportexpress.com); fares for the 20-minute trip cost Rs80, and the trains run from 5am–11pm. You can also travel by pre-paid taxi (Rs350; 45mins), booked at the desk on the arrivals concourse.

Chhatrapati Shivaji International Airport, (BOM; tel: 022-6685 1010; http://www.csia.in) is situated 29km (18 miles) north of the centre of Mumbai. This is by far India's busiest airport, both for international and domestic services; note the international terminal is based over 5km (3 miles) away from the domestic terminal but linked to it by a regular shuttle-bus service. On clear roads the journey downtown takes a little over an hour, but at peak times allow two or three times that. Taxis charge Rs350/450 (non-AC/AC) for the trip. There's also a much cheaper shuttle bus (Rs70; 90mins– 2hrs 30min) which runs from the main terminal to the Air India building on Nariman Point.

Arrival. On arrival you will be required to fill in a Disembarkation Card. Visitors who do not have any dutiable goods, high-value articles, foreign exchange in excess of US$1,000 or unaccompanied baggage, all of which have to be declared, can simply walk through the Green Channel. However, others will have go to the Red Channel for the appropriate clearance.

ALCOHOL

Only one state in India, Mahatma Gandhi's home state of Gujarat, remains completely 'dry', although most regions impose regular 'dry days', particularly during elections. Alcohol is generally available elsewhere, except in very remote areas and in religious centres. Other than luxury hotels, few restaurants are authorised to serve beer or other alcoholic drinks, although many do – don't be surprised if your beer arrives in camouflaged in a teapot, or if you're asked to keep bottles out of sight under the table.

B

BUDGETING FOR YOUR TRIP

The following are some approximate prices in Indian rupees:

Admission charges. Museums in India's metropolitan cities charge a hefty Rs250–300 entry for foreigners (Rs20 for Indians). High ticket prices also affect major sites, notably the Taj Mahal, where overseas tourists pay Rs750 for a one-day pass.

Car hire. Almost all hire cars are chauffeur-driven. In the cities a car may be hired on a flat-rate basis (eg 4 hours or 40km Rs800 non-AC; Rs1,500 AC). For travel outside the cities, count on around Rs2,400–2,700/day for up to 250–300km, and Rs 8–10/km thereafter. More will be charged for a luxury imported vehicle than for an air-conditioned (AC) Indian car. Overnight charges for the driver start from Rs150 to Rs250 per night.

Hotels. Double room in a luxury establishment Rs7,000 to Rs20,000 per night. Mid-range hotels from Rs1,500 to Rs3500 per night for a double, depending on whether it is air-conditioned or not. Local and luxury taxes are extra, approximately 5–20 percent, although this can depend on the state in which you are travelling.

Meals. A three-course evening meal in a mid-range restaurant can cost anywhere between Rs300 and Rs1,000. Eating in a traditional Indian *thali* or 'meals' place, you'll rarely spend more than Rs150–200 for a filling meal of ten or more different dishes, including a dessert. Alcoholic drinks bump up bills considerably, with beer costing from Rs100–250 for a pint bottle. Wine is expensive, at Rs300–1500 for a bottle of Indian origin, and considerably more for imports.

Taxis. Fares to and from airports and major train stations are supposed to operate at a fixed rate. Elsewhere, the driver should use the meter but the usual compromise is to agree a fare before the journey.

Trains. Train from Delhi to Mumbai (approximately 1,400 km/1,000 miles) AC first-class Rs3,305; non-AC couchette Rs449. Indrail Pass: US$270 for 7 days, US$495 for 30 days, US$1,060 for 90 days, first-class AC. Other periods available.

C

CAR HIRE

Indian roads are some of the most difficult and dangerous in the world, and only the most confident (or foolhardy) of foreign drivers venture on them in a self-drive vehicle. It is far more common to book a car with a driver, which can easily be arranged through hotels, tourist offices and reputable travel agents.

CLIMATE

India can be conveniently divided into three zones – the north, the south and the hill regions – and into three distinctive seasons: the winter, the summer and monsoon. The best time to visit India is from mid-September to early April, except for the hill stations, which are good at any time in the summer except during the monsoon.

The following and opposite show average daytime temperatures.

°C		J	F	M	A	M	J	J	A	S	O	N	D
Mumbai	max.	28	28	30	32	33	32	29	29	29	32	32	31
	min.	19	19	22	24	27	26	25	24	24	24	23	21
Kolkata	max.	27	29	34	36	36	33	32	32	32	32	29	26
	min.	13	15	21	24	25	26	26	26	26	24	18	13
Delhi	max.	21	24	31	36	41	39	36	34	34	34	29	23
	min.	7	9	14	20	26	28	27	26	24	18	11	8
Chennai	max.	29	31	33	35	38	38	36	35	34	32	29	29
	min.	19	20	22	26	28	27	26	26	25	24	22	21

CRIME AND SAFETY

Your valuables are probably less at risk in India than in many parts of the West, though commonsense precautions go a long way: don't leave valuables lying around, and avoid being obvious – a few hundred dollars are a year's earnings to many people.

Violence against foreigners is not unknown but it is probably

°F		J	F	M	A	M	J	J	A	S	O	N	D
Mumbai	max.	83	83	86	89	91	89	85	85	85	89	89	87
	min.	67	67	72	76	80	79	77	76	76	76	73	69
Kolkata	max.	80	84	93	97	96	92	89	89	90	89	84	79
	min.	55	59	69	75	77	79	79	78	78	74	64	55
Delhi	max.	70	75	87	97	105	102	96	93	93	93	84	73
	min.	44	49	58	68	79	83	81	79	75	65	52	46
Chennai	max.	85	88	91	95	101	100	96	95	94	90	85	84
	min.	67	68	72	78	82	81	79	78	77	75	72	69

safer to walk through Delhi late at night than many places back home – at least, if you're male. Women should exercise the greatest caution at all times, even in crowded public spaces.

Should you become a victim of crime, seek advice from your guest house or hotel owner about what to do. If you wish to claim on your insurance, you'll need a notification report from the local police.

CUSTOMS

Certain high-value items, such as laptop computers and expensive photographic equipment, may be entered in your passport by customs officials – though this practise is becoming rare these days. Any items that have been written into a passport cannot be sold and must be shown on departure. In case of loss or theft, you will need a police document to prove that you have reported the incident. Firearms and habit-forming drugs are banned and so is the import of gold bullion and electronic items for commercial purposes.

Currency restrictions. It is forbidden to take Indian rupees into or out of the country. There is, however, no limit set on the total amount of foreign currencies that you can bring into India, providing you declare amounts in excess of US$2,500 on arrival. Foreign currencies that total the amount imported and declared may be exported.

Departure. When leaving, you are not allowed to take recognised antiques (items over 99 years old) – it is best to keep your sales receipt with you. You may not export any kind of animal skin other than a small amount of cow leather and a few peacock feathers.

E

ELECTRICITY

Power supply is 220V 50Hz AC, via two- or three-pin round plugs. European visitors should be able to run their appliances using a simple adaptor, widely available locally, while those from the US may also need a transformer.

Supply can be erratic, particularly during the summer months, when air-conditioning units crank into life, massively increasing demand and leading to power cuts. Supply is generally more stable at night.

EMBASSIES, HIGH COMMISSIONS AND CONSULATES

Most countries have diplomatic ties with India, with an embassy or high commission in New Delhi and a consulate in Mumbai, Kolkata or Chennai.

Australia. www.india.embassy.gov.au. *Australian High Commission:* 1/50 G Shantipath, Chanakyapuri, Delhi; tel: 011-4139 9900. *Consulate Generals:* 36 Maker Chambers VI, 220 Nariman Point, Mumbai 400 021; tel: 022-6116 7100

Canada. http://india.gc.ca. *Canadian High Commission:* 7–8 Shantipath, Chanakyapuri, New Delhi 110 021; tel: 011-4178 2000. 6th Floor Fort House, 221 Dr Dn Marg, Mumbai; tel: 022-6749 4444

Ireland. www.irelandinindia.com. *Embassy:* 230 Jor Bagh, New Delhi 110 003; tel: 011-2462 6733

New Zealand. http://new-zealand.visahq.com/embassy/India. *High Commission:* Sir Edmund Hillary Marg, Chanakyapuri, Delhi 110 021; tel: 011-4688 3170. *Consulates:* Level 2, 3 North Avenue, Maker Maxity, Bandra Kurla complex, Mumbai; tel: 022-6131-6668. Maithri, 132 Cathedral Road, Chennai 600 086; tel: 044-2811 2472

UK. http://ukinindia.fco.gov.uk/en. *British High Commission:* Shantipath, Chanakyapuri, New Delhi 110 021; tel: 011-2419 2100. *British*

Deputy High Commissions: Naman Chambers, C/32 G Block Bandra Kurla Complex, Bandra (East) Mumbai 400 051, tel: 022-6650 2222; 1A Ho Chi Minh Sarani, Kolkata 700071, tel: 033-2288 5172; 20 Anderson Road, Chennai 600 006, tel: 044-4219 2151; Ms. Shilpa Caldeira, Head of Consular Section, 303–304 Casa del Sol, Opposite Marriott Hotel Miramar, Panaji; tel: 0832-246 1110

US. http://mumbai.usconsulate.gov *Embassy:* Shantipath, Chanakyapuri, New Delhi 110 021; tel: 011-2419 8000; http://newdelhi.us embassy.gov. *Consulate Generals:* 5/1 Ho Chi Minh Sarani, Kolkata 700071, tel: 033-3984 2400, http://kolkata.usconsulate.gov; Gemini Circle, Chennai 600 006, tel: 044-2857 4000, http://chennai.usconsulate.gov; C-49, G-Block, Bandra Kurla Complex, Bandra East, Mumbai 400051, tel: 022-2672 4000.

ETIQUETTE

All transactions and most social encounters in India begin with the well-established ritual of exchanging visiting cards. Like everywhere else, politeness in India is considered to be a virtue. You'll quickly find that most Indians will go out of their way to be friendly and helpful. A traveller will frequently be asked about his or her nationality, name, marital status and children.

No topics of conversation are taboo, providing you don't take up an intransigent or arrogant stand. On the contrary, Indians are eager to explain their country and beliefs to foreigners.

Indians increasingly shake hands when greeting people, especially during the course of official business; in formal situations a traditional *namasté* with both hands brought together at face level and a slight bow is considered polite.

Many Indians do not drink and/or are vegetarian, so if you are inviting someone out for a meal, it would be a good idea to inquire beforehand about tastes and preferences.

In many places you might find yourself surrounded by swarms of children clamouring for 'school pens and coins' – by ignoring their pleas you will help discourage such pestering.

G

GAY AND LESBIAN TRAVELLERS

Despite a recent relaxation in the law (gay sex is no longer illegal in India), homosexuality is still a taboo subject. While general attitudes are discriminatory, things are changing slowly, and at least the issue of gay and lesbian rights is starting to be discussed, due in no small part to regular depiction of gay and lesbian relationships in Bollywood movies – something which the Hindu hard right firmly opposes.

However, gay and lesbian travellers should be discreet and avoid any public displays of affection (as should heterosexual couples). On the plus side, hotels will think nothing of two men or women sharing a room.

Published in Mumbai, *Bombay Dost* is a magazine that supports gay, lesbian, bisexual and transgender communities throughout the country and its listings pages are a useful resource for nightlife.

GETTING THERE

By air. Most international visitors arrive in Delhi and Mumbai; other international flights serve Kolkata, Chennai, Bengaluru, Thiruvananthapuram, Cochin, Kozhikode and Hyderabad. **Security** checks at airports are particularly intensive in India. Check in at least 3 hours ahead of departure time for international flights, and 2 hours in advance for domestic ones.

By road and train. It is possible to cross into India by land from both Nepal and Bangladesh, but the journey can be somewhat strenuous – by bus from Kathmandu to Delhi, or by bus from Dhaka to the Bangladesh border, then by train to Kolkata. Both routes take a minimum of two or three days. The border with Pakistan is often closed, and the bus and train service between Amritsar, Delhi and Lahore can be suspended without warning.

GUIDES AND TOURS

Specialist India tour operators offer a wide range of tours, from the standard trips of varying lengths to tailor-made itinieraries. Prices vary according to the grade of accommodation you opt for, whether you travel as part of a group or with your own car and driver, and the time of year. Note also, that a good deal of money may be saved by choosing an India-based operator and arranging your own flight. They won't be ATOL or ABTA bonded, offering little protection in the event of cancellation, but your insurance policy should cover such eventualities in any case.

Aadi Kerala, Tel: 0484-266 4256, www.keralatravelagent.in
Audley, Tel: 01933-838000, www.audleytravel.com
Cox & Kings, Tel: 0845-867 2349, www.coxandkings.co.uk
Exodus, Tel: 0845-287 7249, www.exodus.co.uk
TransIndus, Tel: 0484-879 3960, www.transindus.co.uk
Western & Oriental, Tel: 020-7666 1234, www.wandotravel.com

H

HEALTH AND MEDICAL CARE

Before travelling to India, you are advised to take out a personal health insurance policy and consult your doctor for a routine check-up; you could ask them to prescribe medication for potential stomach upsets and you may also need to start a course of anti-malarial drugs before leaving home.

Most people during the course of their stay in India will contract some form of stomach trouble. In most cases, it is nothing to worry about, being more irritating than anything else. The remedy is simple: refrain from eating for 12–24 hours, drink only sterilized water, ideally enriched with rehydration salts. Once the diarrhoea has stopped you can begin to take food again, but stick to boiled rice and yoghurt for the first day, supplemented with banana and chapattis or dry toast the day after. If the loose motion or vomiting lasts for more than 36 hours you should consider seeing a doctor.

Tap water, even in big cities such as Delhi and Mumbai, should always be considered as suspect. However, bottled water is widely available, even in remote areas. If you find yourself having run out, purify your water with a chemical steriliser such as chlorine or silver nitrate, use a dedicated water filter, or else boil it for at least four minutes. Note that apart from in five-star hotels, ice cubes are not usually made with sterilized water and should thus be avoided.

Sensitive skin also needs to be protected against the sun. High levels of heat can cause outbursts of prickly heat (use talcum powder) and migraines. Take plenty of liquids to combat dehydration.

Although not mandatory, vaccinations against typhoid, tuberculosis, hepatitis and tetanus may be worth it. A valid yellow fever certificate is mandatory for those arriving from South America, Africa and other areas where yellow fever exists.

While in India, steer completely clear of stray mammals – particularly dogs – because there is a risk of rabies.

Cities like Delhi and Mumbai have Western-style clinics; your embassy in New Delhi can recommend one. Government hospitals are cheap, but not always as hygienic as those you might be used to at home, so if you are going to have injections done, insist that the doctor either uses a disposable needle or that the sterilisation process is carried out in front of you; this is for your own peace of mind.

Pharmacies are ubiquitous in India, and very cheap.

I'm not feeling well. **mai kuchch bimar hu**
I need a doctor. **mujko doctor chaiyé**
Please give me some water. **mujko pani dijiyé**

L

LANGUAGE

Hindi is the official national language of India, but each state also has its own regional language – one of the 22 listed in the Constitution. English is still used alongside Hindi for official purposes.

People in north India generally speak Hindi, while in the south, where the regional languages are Dravidian, you will find more English spoken.

The following are some useful words and expressions in Hindi. Verbs ending with a 'yé' sound are polite imperatives, but those ending with an 'o' are familiar forms of address. The 'ji' suffix is a polite honorific.

yes **ji ha**

no **nahi**

please **meher bani**

thank you **dhanyavad** (sometimes **'shukriya'** in northern India)

My name is…. **Mera nam… hai**

What is your name? **Apka nam kya hai?**

I beg your pardon/sorry **Maf** (or **shama**) **kijiyé**

hello/welcome/goodbye **namasté**

How are you? **Kya hal hai/ap kaisé hai**

I'm fine. **Thik hai**

I don't understand. **Samjha nahi**

tomorrow/yesterday **kal** (confusion is possible)

today **aj**

tonight **aj rat ko**

good **achcha**

excellent/well done **shabash**

Please go away. **Jaiyé**

Go away! **Jao**

Let's go! **Chalo** (polite form **chaliyé**)

It is very hot. **Bahut garam hai**

It is very cold. **Bahut thanda hai**

It is very beautiful. **Yé bahut sunder hai**

It is very good. **Bahut achcha hai**

This is not good. **Yé achcha nahi hai**

This is not clean. **Yé saf nahi hai**

Numbers

1 **ek**
2 **do**
3 **tin**
4 **char**
5 **panch**
6 **chhé**
7 **saat**
8 **aat**
9 **nau**
11 **gyarah**
10 **dass**
12 **barah**
20 **bis**
30 **tis**
40 **chaalis**
50 **pachas**
60 **sath**
70 **sattar**
80 **assi**
90 **nabbé**
100 **sau**
1,000 **hazar**

The following two numbers are fairly important since they are not only typically Indian but also occur in the press, and on official documents, etc.

100,000 **lakh** (written: 1,00,000)
10,000,000 **crore** (written: 1,00,00,000)

The following are some useful expressions in Tamil:

hello	**vanakkam**
goodbye	**poyvituvarukiren**
yes	**amam**
no	**illai**
thank you	**nandri**
What is your name?	**Ungal peyar yenna?**
My name is…	**Yen peyar…**
Where is…?	**…yenge?**

M

MAPS

Good road maps of the Indian subcontinent are published in Europe; street maps are not always available even in India; your best bet will be the local tourist office or your hotel reception desk. Street maps of big cities like Delhi and Mumbai can be bought from newspaper stands. But by far the most accurate source, at least for street plans if not individual sites, is Google Maps, which is easily accessible via both iOS and Android systems.

MEDIA

Newspapers and magazines. There are a massive number of newspapers available in India, but very few of them have any real journalistic merit. The most popular are the *Times of India* and the *Hindustan Times*, although the *The Hindu* is widely regarded as the most cerebral. There are several local worthwhile *Time/Newsweek* equivalents, including *Outlook*, *India Today* and *Frontline*. while *Tehelka*, is a weekly newspaper dedicated to investigative journalism. For entertainment listings, the best bets are the Entertainments pages of regional editions of the Times of India and Time Out, which publishes separate versions for Delhi, Mumbai and Bengaluru (www.timeoutindia.net). **Radio and TV.** All India Radio (AIR) broadcasts on medium wave, with news either in English, Hindi or a regional language.

As well as the somewhat dull and dated government-run television stations, India hosts more than 150 satellite and cable channels, both local and international, which are available in most hotels. BBC World and CNN are invariably on offer, along with MTV and dozens of Bollywood channels.

MONEY

Currency. The Indian unit of currency is the *rupee* (abbreviated *Rs*), which is divided into 100 *paise*. There is a 50-paise coin, and coins of 1, 2 and 5 rupees. Banknotes exist in denominations of 2, 5, 10, 20, 50, 100, 500 and 1,000 rupees.

Indians are rather fussy about the condition of their paper notes, so check your change carefully every time you pay for something, and refuse any frayed and dirty notes. Don't try to mend notes with transparent sticky tape – they become unacceptable this way.

There is a chronic shortage of small cash and many shopkeepers give out sweets or stamps by way of change. Taxi and auto-rickshaw drivers are also notoriously without adequate change; you might often find yourself having to pay a little more just to break up a roadside deadlock. When cashing in your foreign exchange in a large bank, it would therefore be a good idea to ask to have part of your Indian money given to you in small notes. Some banks give extremely valuable wads of small change. Hang on to the bank receipts, since you may well need them when booking train or air tickets. Note that it is a criminal offence to change money on the black market.

Debit and credit cards and personal cheques. Use and acceptability of debit and credit cards is becoming increasingly widespread. All big hotels and government emporiums recognise them; as do many shops and restaurants, although shops will often add a surcharge over the cash rate if you pay by card. ATMs are attached to most banks, normally in guarded, air-conditioned rooms and in most towns and cities. Check on your bank's transaction charges prior to departure, and be sure to inform them that you're about to visit India so that they don't block your card as a security measure on your first foreign withdrawal or purchase.

Travellers' cheques can be cashed in at most banks and in many hotels, though in the latter case it may be at a slightly inferior rate. Some shops are also authorised to deal in foreign exchange.

money **paisa**
How much is it? **Kya dam hai**
It is very expensive. **Yé bahut mahinga hai**

O

OPENING TIMES

All central government offices follow a five-day week, closing on Saturdays and Sundays. Most **markets** close one day a week; the day varies from place to place. **Shops** generally open at 10am and close by 8pm; some are shut for lunch. Administrative **offices** (other than central railway and airline offices) only start becoming active by about 11am; they will be devoid of life by 5.30pm. The official lunch break is from 1.30 to 2pm. Station booking-counters open with the first trains. **Banks** dealing with foreign currency open from 10.30am to 2.30pm on weekdays, and from 10.30am to 12.30pm on Saturdays. However, on Saturdays it may be difficult to change your travellers' cheques outside the main cities. **Post offices** open at 9.30am, closing at 5.30pm in larger places and 3.30pm elsewhere. **Museums** and **parks** are open until 5 or 5.30pm, but don't necessarily open every day.

P

PHOTOGRAPHY

Digital photography is fast becoming the norm in India, and you find photographic shops equipped with card readers where you can upload and back up your images in most towns and tourist resorts. For a small fee they'll also burn the data onto discs. Colour and black-and-white print film is readily available in the main cities, but professional film stock is only available in the big four gateway cities.

There are certain things that cannot be photographed: military installations, bridges of all sorts, airports and railway stations, power stations and refineries, dams and telephone exchanges. Likewise, it is always best to get permission to photograph any person. Bear in mind, too, that women are generally much happier being photographed by other women than by men.

POLICE

Indian police have earned a reputation for being incorrigibly corrupt. As a foreigner, any dealings with the police – such as reporting thefts of valuables or a passport – are likely to involve requests for a small bribe – Rs200–300 rupees should suffice to oil the wheels. Should you be arrested for any reason, contact your consulate at the first opportunity.

POST OFFICES

The postal service within India and abroad is generally slow and unreliable. An airmail letter usually takes up to 10 days to Europe or the US. Stamps are sold at post offices and in some large hotel receptions. It is best to watch your letters being franked rather than using public letterboxes. Lower denomination stamps and envelopes tend not to stick very well, hence the pot of glue on all counters. You can send bulkier souvenirs home by surface mail, but you must first have the package cleared by customs. The Speed Post service within India is quick (most letters are delivered within 24 hours), cheaper than a courier, and more reliable than standard post. This service is also available for sending letters and parcels to a few foreign countries (destinations vary from one post office to another). More reliable than the Indian postal service are international courier services, available in larger towns and cities.

PUBLIC HOLIDAYS

Due to the many religions in India, public holidays are plentiful and confusing. Fixed national holidays are set on the following dates: 26 January, Republic Day; 15 August, Independence Day; 2 October, Mahatma Gandhi's Birthday; and 25 December, Christmas Day. Banks are closed on 30 September and 31 March. Other holidays vary according to region. A list of official holidays can be obtained from tourist offices.

R

RELIGION

No other country in the world has such a wealth of faiths as India, reflected in the religious activities of its people and the beautiful architecture of its churches, mosques and shrines.

Access to places of worship is generally open, except for some Hindu temples and all Parsi fire-temples. Mosques are closed to non-Muslims at certain times of day. In most places of worship you will be asked to take off your shoes and/or cover your head, so it might be a good idea to take along some form of head-covering. Jain temples forbid anyone entering the premises to bring in any form of leather (including wallets). Therefore, if you wish to take advantage of all the opportunities for sightseeing, you should consider packing a hip bag or money belt made from canvas or another fabric that would be acceptable.

Synagogues can be found in big cities such as Mumbai and Delhi; Christian churches of a variety of denominations exist in practically every town.

S

SMOKING

There's a national ban on smoking in public places, such as offices and railway stations, though in practice this is rarely enforced. The Sikh religion forbids smoking, so you will be asked to hand in all your tobacco at the entrance when visiting a *gurdwara* (Sikh temple).

T

TELEPHONES

India boasts a modern, efficient telephone system. You can make long-distance and international calls direct from most hotel rooms via their landline. Mobile coverage is excellent and improving all the time. For short trips, you may as well stick to your own phone, though check call charges in advance with your service provider – they're invariably extortionate. Mobile calls from Indian SIM cards are considerably cheaper, but getting hold of one can be a time-consuming process: you have to fill in a form, and submit it via a cell phone retailer with passport photos, then wait a minimum of three days.

TIME ZONES

Indian Standard Time (IST) is GMT plus 5.5 hours, winter and summer alike. The most bizarre time difference in the world exists between India and Nepal: 15 minutes!

	New York	London	**Delhi**	Sydney
January	1.30am	6.30am	**noon**	5.30pm
July	2.30am	7.30am	**noon**	4.30pm

TIPPING

It is customary to leave a tip of about 10 percent of the total bill in restaurants. However, tipping elsewhere is entirely discouraged by the Government of India. Do not try to tip government employees, although museum guides will invariably give hints at the end of a conducted tour, so it will be up to you to decide whether his stories and information are worthy of a tip. However, in temples it's a different story: the 'baksheesh' is more or less mandatory. You should also give a couple of rupees to the person who looked after your shoes while you were visiting.

TOILETS

Despite improvements in recent years, the toilets in India are generally very, very basic. Outside hotels, traditional squat-style loos tend to be the norm; on the whole they're a lot smellier. In smarter places there'll be a jet wash on the end of a wall-mounted flex to wash your bottom with; more run-of-the-mill loos will have only a dripping tap with plastic jug for sluicing.

TOURIST INFORMATION

Indian tourist offices will help prepare your trip. The official website is www.incredibleindia.org

Australia: Level 5, Glasshouse Shopping Complex, 135 King Street, Sydney, New South Wales 2000; tel: 02-92219555, e-mail info@india-tourism.com.au

Canada: 60 Bloor Street (West), #1003, Toronto, Ontario M4W 3B8; tel: 416-962-3787; email: indiatourism@bellnet.ca

UK: 7 Cork Street, London W1S 3LH; tel: 020-7437 3677; email: info@indiatouristoffice.org

US: 3550 Wilshire Boulevard, Suite #204, Los Angeles, CA 90010 , tel: 213-380 8855, email: indiatourismindla@aol.com; Suite 1808, 1270 Avenue of the Americas, New York, NY 10020, tel: 212- 586 4901, email: rd@itonyc.com

In India the major tourist offices are:

Mumbai: 123 Maharishi Karve Road, opposite Churchgate; tel: 022-2203 3144/45

Chhatrapati Shivaji Airport: Domestic tel: 022-2615 6920; International tel: 022-2832 5331

Kolkata: 4 Shakespeare Sarani; tel: 033-2282 1402. Dum Dum Airport; tel: 033-2513 0495

Chennai: 154 Anna Salai; tel: 044-2846 0285

Meenambakam Domestic Airport; tel: 044-2256 0386

Delhi: 88 Janpath, New Delhi 110001; tel: 011-2332 0005

Indira Gandhi International Airport; tel: 011-2569 1171

Domestic Airport; tel: 011-2567 5296

Airport tourist offices are open 24 hours a day; others 9am to 6pm.

TRANSPORT

By air (see page 64). Don't waste time on arrival: book as soon as you know where you are going and how you want to get there. There are two types of ticket: *confirmed*, which are (mostly) trouble-free, and *requested* (or *wait-listed*), which frequently offer only a slim chance of travel.

There has been a massive explosion in the number of domestic airlines operating in India over recent years – it's not unusual to find three or four different airlines competing for custom on the busier routes, so it's always worth shopping around the various websites to compare fares and look out for special promotional offers.

The following are the major domestic airlines: Air India (www.airindia.com); Air India Express (www.airindiaexpress.in); Go Air (www.goair.in); IndiGo (http://book.goindigo.in); Jet Airways (www.jetairways.com); Jet Konnect (www.jetkonnect.co.in); Spicejet (www.spicejet.com).

By rail. Indian Railways (www.indianrail.gov.in) have seven basic classes of travel: First Class Air Conditioned (AC), Second Class AC, Third Class AC, AC Chair, First Class non-AC, Second Class Sleeper (non-AC) and Second Class Unreserved. During the summer months an AC compartment is best, especially if travelling through the Indian plains.

All overnight trains have sleepers. Second Class Unreserved seats are wooden planks; First and Second Class and AC berths are cushioned. Second Class berths, whether AC or not, give straight onto the main corridor, but First Class berths are separate compartments with slide-doors and catch-locks. In First Class and Second Class AC, you are provided with sheets and blankets (nights can be chilly in AC, even in the summer).

There are various basic types of train. The best are the 'super-fast' inter-city services; these include the comfortable 'Rajdhani' expresses (which connect Delhi with cities India-wide) and 'Shatabdi' expresses (daytime services linking major cities within eight hours of one another). Other long-distance services are called 'Express' or 'Mail'. Avoid the excruciatingly slow 'Passenger' trains, which stop absolutely everywhere.

Indrail Passes are available, abroad or in India, for various periods of up to 90 days. Tourists are expected to pay for their tickets in foreign exchange.

Since the introduction of a computerised reservation system, booking tickets has become a lot faster and easier. That said, you should aim to obtain your ticket as far in advance as possible. Major stations in Delhi, Mumbai, Kolkata and Chennai have dedicated Tourist Reservation Counters, which speed up the whole process considerably for those with foreign passports; tickets purchased at them always have to be paid for in foreign currency, with travellers' cheques or with cash backed by an encashment certificate from an Indian bank or ATM. Foreigners need their passports for booking tickets.

It's also now theoretically possible to book tickets online at www.irctc.co.in, and more streamlined private sites such as www.cleartrip.com, using foreign credit or debit cards, meaning that you can sort out your train tickets before you even arrive in India. However, in practise, IR requires proof of nationality and residence before accepting any payments, for which you have to post a photocopy of your passport to India, then wait for them to reply with a booking code – all of which generally takes upwards of a fortnight. The most convenient alternative for anyone wishing to secure a booking before arriving in India is to purchase an Inrail pass in your home country – even if only for a maximum period of one day, covering your day of travel. Apart from enabling you to book well in advance, an Inrail pass will also gain you access to special tourist quotas, so you'll nearly always be guaranteed a seat, even on over-subscribed routes. In the UK, Inrail passes may be purchased exclusively through SD Enterprises Ltd, 103, Wembley Park Drive, Wembley, Middlesex HA9 8HG (Tel: 0208-9033411, www.indiarail.co.uk).

Food is served on Indian trains. However, apart from one or two luxury trains, there won't be much of a choice (generally it will be a question of vegetarian or non-vegetarian). Meals will consist of a thali or a cardboard box filled with plastic bags of curry and rice.

India also has a number of **special trains:** the Palace on Wheels (www.rtdc.in), India's original and most famous luxury train, which runs from Delhi around the highlights of Rajasthan in 8 days; Royal Rajasthan On Wheels (www.royalrajasthanonwheels.com), a lavishly appointed locomotive that follows a similar route around Rajasthan, only with a detour east to Varanasi via the temples at Khajuraho; Maharaja's Express, an über-luxurious alternative to the Palace on Wheels offering weekly departures on a range of five inter-city routes across India; the Indian Maharaja (www.theindianmaharaja.co.in), which travels from Mumbai to Delhi via the famous cave sites of Ellora and Ajanta, then on to Udaipur, Ranthambore tiger reserve and Jaipur in Rajasthan, before stopping at Agra en route to Delhi; the Deccan Odyssey (www.deccan-odyssey-india.com), which starts in Mumbai, but heads south down the Konkan coast to Goa, before swinging north again through Kolhapur to Aurangabad, for Ellora and Ajanta Caves; and the Golden Chariot (www.thegoldenchariot.co.in), which takes in the highlights on the southern Indian state of Karnataka.

By road. Where there is no railway (eg in the Himalayas), there will be a road and dozens of inter-city buses. The fares are low, and so is the comfort. Buses on major routes are plush and classy.

Discovering India by car is more comfortable but the best advice to anyone who is thinking about driving in India is: don't. Roads can be very congested and dangerous and there are many unwritten rules followed by other drivers. It is far better, and cheaper, to hire a car with chauffeur. However, if you do have to drive you will need your domestic licence, liability insurance, an international driver's permit and your vehicle's registration papers.

Urban public transport. Kolkata and Delhi have **metro** lines (both are clean and cool). In all big cities there is an efficient **bus** service which, when you know how to use the route guide available from all bookstalls, is convenient. The only problem is that buses in India carry large crowds and are not always well driven.

Taxis abound in all large cities. Drivers should agree to use the meter, converting the reading at the end of your journey with a 'rate card'. However, they may be reluctant to do so and in practice it's easier to haggle a fare in advance.

Auto-rickshaws (three-wheel mini-taxis) operate in a similar way to taxis. Again, fare rates vary from town to town; in general, an auto-rickshaw fare is about half a normal taxi fare. Always fix fares in advance, which may involve haggling. Auto-rickshaws are banned in Mumbai's congested inner-city zone (and from the airports), so you must use a taxi, bus or suburban train.

There are also **cycle-rickshaws** and *tongas* (horse-drawn carts), for which you agree on the price before starting off.

Are you free? (taxi, rickshaw) **Kya ap khali hai**
How far is it? **Kitni dur hai**
Where is it? **Kaha hai**
On your right **Day**
On your left **Bay**
Straight ahead **Sidha**
Please stop here. **Yaha rokiyé**
Please go faster. **Jaldi chaliyé**
Please go slowly. **Dhiré chaliyé**

VISAS AND PERMITS

All visitors to India require a visa, apart from nationals of Nepal and Bhutan.

Transit visas, with a maximum duration of 15 days, are only needed if you are simply making a stop-over and want to leave the airport. They are granted to passengers who have tickets for onward destinations. Two-way transit visas can also be obtained.

Tourist visas are normally valid for six months. It's virtually impossible to extend a tourist visa – you have to travel to a neighbouring country and apply for a new one. You must arrive in India within six months of the visa date of issue, or it will automatically become void. For a tourist visa, you will need two passport-size photos (check the exact size before submitting the form as it tends to be an irregular one). Unless you hold a passport from a fee-exempt country, you will be expected to pay for your tourist visa. Tour organisers can arrange for group visas. Application forms may be downloaded from the Indian High Commission or Consulate website in your own country. You fill them in online and print off a copy to be posted, along with the requisite fee and photographs.

Full information on the application process for an Indian visa is featured at: http://in.vfsglobal.co.uk

Other entry permits. Most of India is open to foreign travel, but special permits have to be obtained to visit certain parts of Arunachal Pradesh, Mizoram, Nagaland, Manipur, Sikkim and some islands, including the Andaman Islands.

Some of these areas are open only to organised tours, not to individual tourists; time limits on visits also apply in some cases. Information on restrictions and permits should be obtained from your local Indian tourist office or Indian embassy in advance of your trip.

W

WHAT TO BRING

Pack a cloth hat to protect against the sun, as well as sensible light cotton clothes to wear during the hot and monsoon seasons, a swimsuit and a warm top for cold spells during winter or trips to the hills.

Other useful items include: a pocket torch; a padlock if you are thinking of staying in a few cheaper hotels or if you are going to travel a lot on Indian railways; a penknife; water-purifying tablets or pump-action filter, such as the Katadyn Hiker Pro (www.katadyn. com), which keeps you healthy and avoids endless purchases of plastic water bottles; a money belt; and half a dozen passport-size photos of yourself, which will come in useful if you are applying for permits to restricted areas or for a rail pass.

A universal plug for wash basins will come in handy more often than you might imagine. Ear plugs can sometimes be a life-saving device, particularly at night in crowded compartments, or in a bus with non-stop Indian film music (often distorted) blaring out of the public address system. And don't forget chargers for your mobile phone and other electronic devices.

While aspirin and mosquito repellent are readily available a small bottle of light wound disinfectant, some sterile cotton wool and adhesive bandages, something for insect bites, and toilet paper or paper tissues (found only in large Indian towns and tourist resorts) are good things to have in your bag.

WEBSITES AND INTERNET CAFÉS

Some useful websites are:

www.bollywoodworld.com – film news and reviews

www.cleartrip.com – efficient booking and timetable site for trains and planes

http://heritagehotels.com – Indian heritage hotel listings

www.incredibleindia.org – official tourism website

www.indiaexpress.com – entertainment news

www.indiamike.com – Indian travel forum

www.timesofindia.com – the newspaper's website

www.transindus.com – recommended specialist travel agent for India

For a huge country where telephone charges are relatively high and postal services unreliable, the internet has provided an inexpensive and popular means for people to keep in touch, and as a result you'll find 'Internet Booths', cafés and computer terminals in all but the most remote villages. Many places are now equipped with fast ADSL or broadband lines although in smaller and more remote places, erratic dial-up connections are still the norm. Rates vary from state to state, anything from Rs20 to Rs70 per hour.

INDEX

Berlitz pocket guide

India

Sixth Edition 2013

Written by Jack Altman
Updated by David Abram
Edited by Sarah Sweeney
Art Editor: Jo Mercer
Series Editor: Tom Stainer
Production: Tynan Dean and Rebeka Ellam

Photography credits: Abe Nowitz/Apa Publications 131, 133, 135, 136, 210; AKG 49, 50; Apa Publications 175; Bill Wassman/Apa Publications 15, 199; Britta Jaschinski/Apa Publications 2MC, 6TL, 7MC, 10, 16, 18, 22, 62, 64, 65, 159, 161, 163, 164, 181, 182, 186, 194, 200, 202, 206, 208, 211, 213, 215, 220; Corbis 37, 38, 43, 46, 54, 56, 59, 105; David Abram/Apa Publications 2TL, 151, 155, 156, 198, 225; Dreamstime 4ML, 4ML, 25, 103; Henry Wilson/Apa Publications 1, 5MC, 13, 52, 68, 71, 73, 76; iStockphoto 2TC, 2ML, 4TL, 4/5M, 6ML, 7MC, 7TC, 26, 33, 41, 45, 98, 101, 102, 106, 108, 110, 112, 113, 115, 116, 117, 119, 120, 123, 124, 126, 128, 129, 142, 147, 148, 150, 153, 167, 170, 185, 192; Julian Love/Apa Publications 3T, 3M, 4TL, 5T, 5TC, 8, 11, 14, 20, 67, 78, 81, 82, 84, 87, 88, 92, 94, 96, 205, 214, 219, 226; Walter Imber/Apa Publications 3TC, 2/3M, 2/3M, 2/3M, 6ML, 28, 30, 34, 74, 89, 91, 114, 134, 139, 140/141, 144, 157, 166, 168, 172, 177, 179, 189, 190, 195, 196, 222
Cover picture: Corbis

Contact us

At Berlitz we strive to keep our guides as accurate and up to date as possible, but if you find anything that has changed, or if you have any suggestions on ways to improve this guide, then we would be delighted to hear from you.
Berlitz Publishing, PO Box 7910,
London SE1 1WE, England.
email: berlitz@apaguide.co.uk
www.insightguides.com/berlitz